Let's Move

Mountains

Andrew Feehily

ISBN: 0-9761796-0-1

BOOKS WRITTEN BY THE AUTHOR: ANDREW FEEHILY.

People Buy People.
Managing The Hurdles.
Bringing Business Ideas To Life.

Website

www.letsmovemountains.com

3 John 2

"Beloved, I wish above all things that thou mayest prosper and be in health, even as thy soul prospereth."

WELCOME 4
Let's Move Mountains.

CHAPTER ONE 7
Words Are Life Itself.

CHAPTER TWO 29
Believe You Can Succeed & You Will.

CHAPTER THREE 46
Spiritual Roadblocks.

CHAPTER FOUR 65
Structure For Success.

CHAPTER FIVE 83
God & Prophecies.

CHAPTER SIX 122
Life Changing Scriptures.

CHAPTER SEVEN 136
Move Mountains With Prayer.

Welcome To Let's Move Mountains

I am Andrew Feehily the author of the book, which has been inspired from God's good book. "The Bible."

I was born in Derbyshire, England in 1964 and named Andrew by my mother Patricia who was also born in England within a small village called Penkridge. My mother named my brothers and I from the names of the disciples in the Bible, being a Christian believer in God. My father Michael was born in Ireland and left his Catholic up bringing at the age of 15 to chase his own dreams in England were he was destined to meet my mother. Over the years, God has worked sometimes the impossible for me. So one of the main advantages of "Lets Move Mountains" is to provide you with a way to understand the impact that the Bible has on all of our lives, including how God can help to improve a quality of life for all of us. The hardest part in today's society is to include God within our daily personal and business life. I hope that by reading this book you too can have a better understanding in your walk with God, knowing that our Spiritual Father wants to share in all our endeavors.

My objective to achieve will be to demonstrate that God has plans for all our lives whilst we are living on this earth. As I keep reading the King James Bible, I realized that everything that I have achieved, or failed through my life at home and at work, has in one form or another been mentioned in the Bible scriptures, just as other people have succeeded, or failed in Gods rewards. I have included a number of my own testimonials that can be related to Biblical scriptures.

"For I know the plans I have for you, "declares the Lord," plans to prosper you and not to harm you, plans to give you hope and a future. Then you will call upon me and come and pray to me, and I will listen to you." **(Jeremiah 29: 11-12).**

What is important, we should be communicating and reading God's written Words during our busy life, in order to succeed for the glory of our Heavenly Father. Before I continue what you need to believe is: There is only one God, the maker of all things, His rightful authority over the world and the Bible in its entirety as inspired by the Word of God. To some of us, it will be a walk into the unknown by discovering that God will provide. God wants us to prosper in living a fulfilling life that is full of real rewards. From a biblical perspective, there are no real ethical standards in this world, unless we demonstrate our walk in obedience to God's Word, so that we can then find a hope for the future through the plans that God has for our lives. Starting today, it is not about finding self-worth anymore, as that plan keeps failing for you. From today, you now have a plan for the future: ***"For I know the plans I have for you, "declares the Lord."*** Work plays a vital role in today's existence; "it is the fruits of our labor that gives us the opportunity to live our lives".

To enjoy the fruits of our labor, we need to be fulfilled in that role. Our own goals and motivation are not enough. We have been given qualities that no other form of life or creation can possibly posses, with powers within us that are waiting to be discovered, with gifts and abilities in performing sometimes the impossible thing. God has created us in his own self-form, noble in reason, wisdom through life, by His thoughts and Words. Many of us have thanked God for our luck and blame him for our failures. We walk many paths to find what we think is the straight path, which always ends up as a crossroad in our lives. The best way for us to understand the plan that God wants for our lives is to allow the scriptures from the Bible to speak for itself.

Gen 1:1 (KJV) ***"In the beginning God created the Heaven and the Earth."*** *John 1:1-4 & 14 (KJV)* ***"In the beginning was the Word, and the Word was with God, and the Word was God. The same was in the beginning with God. All things were made by him; And without him was not anything made that was made. In him was life; and the life was the light of men. And the Word was made flesh, and dwelt among us, and we beheld his glory, the glory as of the only begotten of the Father, full of grace and truth."***

Why did God create you in his own magnificent image, in his substance? Why did God create the world for you to inherit? God gave you this for your first taste, for what will be your inheritance to come. God gave you at no cost, no money down, no lease agreement, and no debt attached, a life to live for the good of our Heavenly Father that wants to shine down on all of His sons and daughters.

CHAPTER ONE

Words Are Life Itself.

CONTROLLING OUR WORDS

This chapter looks at ways for a believer in God to use positive words in our life, against the devices of using negative soul-destroying words.

"*Mark. 11:23.* What You Say Is What You Get."
"Do you see this mountain? If you want to move it, all you have to do is speak to it and if you believe what you say, then you can have it. You can have whatsoever you say."

This scripture has made me realize that we have to truly believe in our Heavenly Father, as He wants us to control our words for positive changes in our life. Throughout today's life and business world, throughout the whole of humankind, words are the beginning and the end of all of our existence. **"Words Create Can Create Positive or Negative Meaning To Our Lives."** The power of words can control our feelings. (To confess it, is to believe it.) Also to control our mouth, is to control our mind. Therefore, what I am saying to you is that our feelings create suggestions in two ways:
POSITIVE OR NEGATIVE.
Our mouth creates suggestions in two ways:
POSITIVE OR NEGATIVES.

Right or wrong words that we use, is the basis for controlling our feelings; so, if we control words we will control our feelings. The most powerful words ever written were made by our own creator, God. Over the centuries of time, the written Word has been used for every conceivable thing throughout life. Words give us the ability to create wisdom, to communicate, to better our existence, in all shapes and forms.

Words can control, dictate, improve, or destroy. I truly believe that all our good positive words are of God that wants to guide us in the path of righteousness and negative words used are of evil, which makes us all fail and effect everything and everyone around us. God wants us to walk in His commandments, to love Him, to fear Him, and to walk in His ways. To fear the Lord is to hate evil, and since His creation, evil has become part of our lifestyle in today's world. We have to use words to convince ourselves to achieve things in life, therefore we must have faith, belief, and obedience to God and understand what the difference is between positive and negative communication. We must realize that God did not make us to suffer. God is a positive force within our lives; therefore, we need to reject negativity within our words. **Words have tremendous power on everybody's life; we react to what we hear or say. Negativity** words will stop us from believing in God, and stops us from receiving our plan, or purposes and our inheritance. It starts with the word's that comes from within us. In our words, we can easily create doubt and fear; therefore, we must not have doubt or fear, as doubt and fear plays a major role in all our lives and can have a negative effect in us prospering further with God. John the Baptist had a tremendous amount of belief; trust and love for God and from his mouth came faith. When he first saw Jesus, he had faith and belief stating, "Look the Lamb of God." When John Baptized Jesus, he saw the heavens open and the spirit came down as a dove and remained on Jesus. When John the Baptist was locked up in Jail and close to being executed, John must have been very fearful, scarred in fear for his life and in doubt as a Christian believer, as he sent his disciples to Jesus asking; are you really the one? (John 1: 29-33) From fear, we can also have great doubt and disbelief. **The Bible says** "Do Not Fear." **Jesus said** "Do Not Fear, Do Not Worry." **Matthew 6:** "Do not have any anxieties, do not have any stress." Therefore, do not allow it in your words. Both f**ear** and f**aith** produce fear in your words, or faith in your words.

So, what are some other devices of negativity or evil?

- **Offense, being offended by others.**

- **Faintness in mind and heart.**

- **Shame-being ashamed of your beliefs.**

- **Unreliability; making others mistrust you.**

There are loads more like lying, cheating, deceiving, and even being shy. All those things will stop us from receiving anything good in your life; it will stop us receiving any form of inheritance, reward, prosperity, or achievements. When you use negative words that you speak in your life; these words will try to get you to lose faith in all your beliefs of God. Good positive words will help you lead a quality life. ***"If a man can control his tongue he can control anything."*** Your Mouth, your words bring increase, or decrease. *"A man's belly shall be satisfied with the fruit of his mouth, and with the increase of lips shall he be filled."* ***(Proverbs: 18:20.)***

"A man shall eat good by the fruit of his mouth, but the soul transgressors shall have violence. He that keepeth his mouth keepeth his life, but he that openeth wide his lips shall have destruction." ***(Proverbs. 13:2,3.)***

In other words do not ***Talk Cheap*** remember to be satisfied by fruits of your mouth, you must ***TALK positive.*** Having faith in what we say is a very powerful tool to recognize in our life. It makes us act straight away on those words. I am sure that everybody, at one time or another, has made a statement, and through faith within our words, it has automatically happened. The words that we say can have a tremendous effect on our lives and people around us. Here are a few examples of being negative in your words. These words will cause us to have disobedient behavior in our life:

OFFENSE: She ignored me; I am not going to talk with her.
SHAME: I don't dress as well as them. They will not accept me.
DOUBT. They didn't buy from me. I am not a good sales person.
GREED: That is mine you can't have any. I do not like to share.
PRIDE: I deserve that position. I am far better than he is.
ENVY: She has all the luck. I will never be that lucky.
VANITY: I am the prettiest here. My friends need to be like me.
JEALOUSY: He has everything so easy. It is hard to me.

Negative words are not God's Creation. The Word of God is positive, as negative words are of the devil. (Any words that are of doubt; must be removed from your vocabulary.) It is said that the devil or evil spirit can move in the same realm as God. The good things about negative words are; they can be weak, leaving space for counter-reaction for positive words. It is important, that you become wise in your words, and be positive that things will be done. You can also be negative in your words and get the same results; *it will be done.* Now, I bet you have heard these statements before, and sure enough, they come to fruition:

- **None of you will ever succeed, unless you listen.**
- **Those kids of mine are getting worse.**
- **I will be late today; I am always late.**
- **I will never succeed in this career.**
- **I hate you, I love you.**

"What comes out of your mouth will determine your future." I remember when I was about five years old; every Sunday afternoon I would sit in front of the television to watch my favorite program. As the evening was approaching, my mother used to say to me. "Come on Andrew get washed, get dressed and be ready to leave for church in twenty minutes." My face would automatically change in to a frown. One Sunday evening, my mother was talking to my grandma: "I don't know what to do about Andrew, he doesn't like church, he would rather sit there in front of the television and watch his favorite program." Sure enough, not only did she say it, it happened, for several weeks without fail until I was disciplined. "Words created our physical body, words are everything. **"Job in the bible said, *"Words will maketh you or breaketh you."***

In the Bible, **Kings 1, Chapter 2, Verse 3.** God is teaching us that the godly person has confidence. That God cares about our character, faithfulness, and integrity; God rewards those who walk in faith with Him. The Lord prospers and grants success to those who walk in his ways.

"***And keep the charge of the LORD thy God, to walk in his ways, to keep his statutes, and his commandments, and his judgments, and his testimonies, as it is written in the law of Moses, that thou mayest prosper in all that thou doest, and whithersoever thou turnest thyself.***"

BUSINESS LOSS THROUGH WORDS

Whether you are in employed as a owner, manager, or a production operator, it is very easy to cover up the truth of a mistake made whilst working, or maybe you rebel against you're team workers, or you make excuses for being late for work, or you procrastinate on a task that needed to be achieved by a certain deadline. Sin runs rampant in today's business world. Christians, like the rest of the world, are often involved in the sin of the world whether through covering up the truth by your words in business; telling white lies, exaggerating the truth, or pretending by telling people that you love the job that you actually hate. I have known people in my passed employment that have passed the buck on to other employees, so that there own creditability stands strong with their superior. I have also seen work colleges lie to customers, when they complain about one of the products and services that was provided in error. All these forms of disobedient behavior patterns will cause short-term gains, and at worse the loss of customer's faith in you, it could lead to you losing your job because they cannot trust a word that you say. Most people believe that since they have made a profession of faith in the Lord Jesus Christ that they will automatically go to Heaven. It is true that anyone who knows Jesus Christ as Lord and Savior will one day be in Heaven; but it is also true that the desire to sin through words, should have been greatly alleviated, when that same person puts their trust in Jesus Christ. I cannot judge who is or who is not saved; but I can make an educated guess by examining their fruits of their mouth. Regardless of whether a person is saved or not, there is still a price to pay for sinful words. We will suffer great loss for our sins whilst we are in this world.

Here are just a few examples, of what we have to lose when we sin through our mouth:

We Have A Loss Of Light.

I have known many people throughout my business career that have lied, or deceived to benefit their careers. I have noticed that people who lie in business, lose their spark as you can see it in their faces as a loss of light, these people are the in the dark struggling for a way out from guilt.

1 John 1:6-7 (KJV) ***"If we say that we have fellowship with him, and walk in darkness, we lie, and do not the truth: But if we walk in the light, as he is in the light, we have fellowship one with another, and the blood of Jesus Christ his Son cleanseth us from all sin."***

Colossians 3:9-10 ***"Lie not one to another, seeing ye have put off the old man with his deeds; And have put on the new man, which is renewed in knowledge after the image of him that created him."***

Proverbs 24:28 ***"Be not a witness against thy neighbour without cause; and deceive not with thy lips."***

Proverbs 12:19 ***"The lip of truth shall be established for ever: but a lying tongue is but for a moment."***

We Have A Loss Of Joy - One of the main objectives that everyone tries to achieve in their life and employment is having joy. Once this has been taken away, our working environment is less- pleasing and we lose sight of the reason why God gave us this opportunity in our life of helping others.

1 John 1:4 (KJV) ***"And these things write we unto you, that your joy may be full."***

John 15:9-11 (KJV) ***"As the Father hath loved me, so have I loved you: continue ye in my love. If ye keep my commandments, ye shall abide in my love; even as I have kept my Father's commandments, and abide in his love. These things have I spoken unto you, that my joy might remain in you, and that your joy might be full."***

If lying is a problem in your life using the following Psalm in prayer to God in restoring back you're joy: Psalms 51:12 (KJV) ***"Restore unto me the joy of thy salvation; and uphold me with thy free spirit."*** Galatians 5:22-23 (KJV) ***"But the fruit of the Spirit is love, joy, peace, longsuffering, gentleness, goodness, faith, Meekness, temperance: against such there is no law."***

When joy is taken out of our employment, it is hard to achieve joy in your employment opportunity that you have been given as a blessing from God. Joy is one of the main ingredients that keep's you employed longer, whereby the fruits of your labor satisfy you.

We Sustain A Loss Of Peace - To have a loss of peace in our working environment causes us to create working issues with our fellow work colleagues. With loss of peace, it is easy to argue and disagree on daily work tasks and cause problems in trying to reach mutual business discussions. In the Bible, it points out what can happen when there is no peace in our working environment.

Isaiah 48:22 (KJV) "***There is no peace, saith the LORD, unto the wicked."***

Ezekiel 7:25 (KJV) ***"Destruction cometh; and they shall seek peace, and there shall be none."*** Psalm 34:14 ***"Depart from Evil, and do good; seek peace, and pursue it."***

John 14:27 ***"Peace I leave with you, my peace I give unto you: not as the world giveth, give I unto you. Let not your heart be troubled, neither let it be afraid."***

Psalm 29:11 ***"The Lord will give Strength unto his people; the Lord will bless his people with peace."***

We Experience A Loss Of Love - Whether a loss of love for your job, or a loss of love for you colleges, your employment is the same as a relationship with a husband or wife. Without love, the working environment that you work in will become strained.

Hebrews 6:10-11 ***"For God is not unrighteous to forget your work and labour of love, which ye have shewed toward his name, in that ye have ministered to the saints, and do minister. And we desire that every one of you do shew the same diligence to full assurance of hope unto the end."***

1 John 4:11-13 (KJV) ***"Beloved, if God so loved us, we ought also to love one another. No man hath seen God at any time. If we love one another, God dwelleth in us, and his love is perfected in us. Hereby know we that we dwell in him, and he in us, because he hath given us of his Spirit."***

1 John 2:3-5 (KJV) ***"And hereby we do know that we know him, if we keep his Commandments. He that saith, I know him, and keepeth not his commandments, is a liar, and the truth is not in him. But whoso keepeth his word, in him verily is the love of God perfected: hereby know we that we are in him."***

We Suffer A Loss Of Fellowship - When we do not meditate on God's Words, or pray for wisdom in the morning and throughout the day, we can easily lose the fellowship of God who guides us positively in words for our working environment.

1 John 1:6-7 (KJV) ***"If we say that we have fellowship with him, and walk in darkness, we lie, and do not the truth: But if we walk in the light, as he is in the light, we have fellowship one with another, and the blood of Jesus Christ his Son cleanseth us from all sin."***

We Lose Confidence – It is easy to lose confidence when we use negative words in our home or at work, as we must then seek the Lords help to give solutions and by seeking God in asking for His guidance, He will then give us the words needed to restore our confidence needed.

John 6:63 ***"It is the spirit that quickeneth; the flesh profiteth nothing: the words that I speak unto you, they are spirit, and they are life."*** Matthew12:37 ***"For by thy words thou shalt be justified, and by thy words thou shalt be condemned."***

What losses will you experience because of your sin? Are you prepared to pay the penalty for your trespasses against God? Are you prepared to not only die because of your sin; but possibly spend an eternity without Him, as lying is one of the major sins of this world.

1 John 1:8-10 (KJV) ***"If we say that we have no sin, we deceive ourselves, and the truth is not in us. If we confess our sins, he is faithful and just to forgive us our sins, and to cleanse us from all unrighteousness. If we say that we have not sinned, we make him a liar, and his word is not in us."***

God wants to share in your life, whether it is in your home or at business - ***"And he will love thee, and bless thee, and multiply thee: he will also bless the fruit of thy womb, and the fruit of thy land, thy corn, and thy wine, and thine oil, the increase of thy kine, and the flocks of thy sheep, in the land which he sware unto thy fathers to give thee."*** **(Deuteronomy 7:13).**

People have always thoroughly fascinated me. Soon after I meet them, I sense that there is something extraordinary about them. They think deeply and intelligently about things and their ideas can be creative and interesting. I find myself asking them questions and listening intently to the answers, as I want to get to know them better by find out what they feel about God, and what makes them the people they are. Getting to know them is helpful to me, but getting to know God, has proved to be the most helpful reason of understanding my life's plan. The more I probed His nature, the more convinced I became in knowing that God is the solution to most of my problems. I became convinced that knowing God better, was the only answer to many of my problems.

***"Know therefore that the LORD thy God, he is God, the faithful God, which keepeth covenant and mercy with them that love him and keep his commandments to a thousand generations;"* (Deuteronomy 7:9.**

"God loves them that love Him; and those that seek Him shall find Him."

***"And we have known and believed the love that God hath to us. God is love; and he that dwelleth love in God, and God in him.* (1 John 4:16)**

Would you say that you know God? Intimately, or maybe personally? If so, how well? Barely or just casually. Today's media reveals that, in spite of the increased population of our society, the majority of Americans still believe in the existence of God.

KNOWING GOD THROUGH HIS WORDS

Most people can also have their doubts by saying through their words; "is there a God?" However, when the person considers the words of the scriptures thoroughly from the evidence in the bible, they conclude that, there is no other logical explanation for things in life, as we know it. Would you then say; is there a personal God? What if I asked people: Do you know God intimately? Many would admit that they had never actually talked about it. Having a personal and intimate relationship with God is something that has never really occurred to most people. In fact, they are not even sure that God is knowable. When you look at the billions of people on this earth, it is estimated that there is 32.9% of the population that are Christian Believers. The rest of the population is made up of non-believers and or of another form of godly belief having our own mental image of what God is like. Psychologists tell us that it is formed largely through our relationships with our earthly fathers. For some, God is an angry tyrant who is upset with them most of the time. For others, God is a strict disciplinarian who is always watching over their shoulders, ready to rap them on the knuckles if they step out of line. Worst still, people can also feel that God is an absent father, who is too busy to care about them, even though He created them. People can sometimes feel He has other important priorities then to listen or try to help. There is not much sense in trying to get to know a god like that.

" ***And it shall come to pass, that before they call, I will answer; and while they are yet speaking, I will hear.*** " **(Isaiah 65:24)**

Most people would like to say that God is on their side, rather than against them, or say that God will be there when they need Him.

I have often wondered what God thinks about all of this? As God is knowable and He does want to be known by telling us that our eternal state depends wholly upon knowing Him and reading His Word in the Bible.

Jesus said: ***"And this is eternal life, that they may know Thee, the only true God, and Jesus Christ whom Thou hast sent"*** **(John 17:3).**

Knowing God and His Son Jesus, is the important aspect relating to eternal life. The above scripture verse does not refer to a casual acquaintance, as it is a message telling us we need to have a personal relationship with God. Therefore, if knowing God is that important, we need to find out how we can draw closer to Him. Some people have not made much of a response in their relationship with God, as they feel that knowing enough about Him is acceptable for their salvation. Unfortunately, it is very easy to get wrapped up in today's life, whereby you have to much going on, and or we listen to others that changes our opinion towards God through their negative words. This can then result in God getting crowded out of your thoughts. Words from others, including yourself will lead to spiritual and emotional depression, ending with a constant sense of loss when times get tough. Things in your life will never really change until you develop a burning desire to know God more intimately. Getting to know God intimately, is the single most important issue in any Christian's life, (in fact any persons life) as it affects so many aspects of our spiritual walk in communicating with our Heavenly Father. For example most believers, who desire to please God, want to know His will. They are normally saying to themselves: What does God want me to do? Knowing God intimately will provide the answer to that question. As our knowledge grows, you will begin to talk and think as if God would, see things as God would see them and have a burden about the same issues God would have for our life.

Once you are at this stage in your relationship with God, you will know the very reason why you searched to grow and cultivate an intimate relationship with God. Moses had a very strong desire in knowing God intimately and He showed Moses favor in talking with him.

"Now therefore, I pray thee, if I have found grace in thy sight, shew me now thy way, that I may know thee, that I may find grace in thy sight:" (Exodus 33:13).

The desire of Moses heart was to truly know God and Moses request, resulted in a great promise from God:

"My presence shall go with you, and I will give you rest." (Exodus 33:14).

This was a beautiful assurance of God's perpetual guidance and care, but that still was not being close enough to God for Moses. With every new revelation God gave to Moses through His Words, it stirred a hunger in his heart for more and with a longing in his soul he cried: ***"I pray Thee, show me Thy glory!"*** *(Exodus 33:18).*

Moses yearned to know all that a human being could possibly absorb about an infinite God and his soul thirsted for further words and knowledge of Him. That is exactly how we need to be in getting to know God, as Moses realized that life in this world was empty and meaningless without God. Moses longed to know God and cried out from the depths of his soul: ***"Show me Thy Glory."*** Any person that is that intense in searching for God's intimacy will be ready for an earthshaking and life changing experience. David the king of Israel, in the Old Testament had the same desire:

"One thing have I desired of the LORD, that will I seek after; that I may dwell in the house of the LORD all the days of my life, to behold the beauty of the LORD, and to enquire in his temple." (Psalm 27: 4). To dwell in the house of the Lord was to live in intimate fellowship with God. ***" As the hart panteth after the water brooks, so panteth my soul after thee, O God. My soul thirsteth for God, for the living God: when shall I come and appear before God?"*** (Psalm 42: 1-2.) The Apostle Paul had the desire as well: (Philippians 8:7-8). ***"But whatever things were gain to me, those things I have counted as loss for the sake of Christ. More than that, I count all things to be loss in view of the surpassing value of knowing Christ Jesus my Lord, for whom I have suffered the loss of all things, and count them but rubbish in order that I may gain Christ."***

All the position, praise, power, prestige and possessions of earth was like city's trash to Paul compared to the relationship of knowing and talking Godly words with Jesus. The overpowering passion of Paul's life was to know Christ That was the main reasons why God used him so powerfully. Asking God to give you that same desire will help you cultivate a thirst for Him. Then you will want to read more of God's Words in the Bible, and then God will start to share with you his plans for your life. With the revelations that you receive from God, will create a desire and a thirst to know more by accepting what God Reveals. When God reveals Himself, you will have an overwhelming sense of joy and peace, with a secure feeling for your well-being. When you hear the words of negative talking people shunning God, or express anger words towards God, your hearts will be saddened. These are typical emotions of our love for God knowing that He is in us. Therefore, we must conduct our lives that will be pleasing to God in a manner, consistent with the words that we read in the Bible and the words that we talk.

GOD USES ORDINARY PEOPLE IN SPREADING HIS WORD

As you read God's words in the Bible, you will automatically recognize that; God uses what most would class as ordinary people to accomplish great things for Him and that is whom God uses to accomplish His Work right here on this earth for your calling. Not many wise, not many mighty, not many noble people are called according to the flesh. God has chosen you, as you have searched for Him.

"No flesh should glory in His presence, he who glories, let him glory in the Lord."

"For ye see your calling, brethren, how that not many wise men after the flesh, not many mighty, not many noble, are called: But God hath chosen the foolish things of the world to confound the wise; and God hath chosen the weak things of the world to confound the things which are mighty; And base things of the world, and things which are despised, hath God chosen, yea, and things which are not, to bring to nought things that are: That no flesh should glory in his presence. But of him are ye in Christ Jesus, who of God is made unto us wisdom, and righteousness, and sanctification, and redemption: That, according as it is written, He that glorieth, let him glory in the Lord. **(1 Corinthians 1:26-31.)**

God also tells us that each one of us is a special creation of His. No one else is just like you. Your physical appearance, your voice, your personality traits, your habits, intelligence, and personal tastes. All of these make you one of a kind. Even your fingerprints distinguish you from every other human being. God out of love and caring for all of us sent His Son, the Lord Jesus Christ, to open the door to an Eternal Relationship with Him. He did this so that we might become spiritually unique people that can be used in accomplishing His work and Will as we place our lives in His hands. God uses people who will give their all, no matter how small your ALL may seem to you, because little becomes much when you place it in the hands of God. When yielded to the touch of God's loving Words, you will then understand how your life can never be the same. God uses just ordinary people like you and me. Your life will never be the same, as your love in His Words will compel you even closer to Him.

"If the Lord delights in a man's ways, He makes his steps firm, though he stumbles, he will not fall, for the Lord upholds him with His hand." (Psalm 37:23-24.)

Then, knowing what lies ahead for you, it is unlikely that you won't become bored with being a Christian, nor become spiritually dull and indifferent; but you will be anxious to read more on God's Words, by following the example of those who receive all that God has promised them through His Words. By being intimate with God, you will have to be strong in your words for faith and love in building an intimate relationship with God.

UNDERSTANDING THE MYSTERY OF GOD'S WORD.

We must trust in God, that He will leads us all to a better understanding of life through His Words, that will in time lead to a life that is pleasing to Him. Our Almighty God has given us the wisdom through the words of life and with this wisdom from His Words; we should recognize the will of God for our lives; and with these words of wisdom, we the servants need to obey the truth of His Words. By obeying the truth of God's Words, we can surpass everything else, for we are also the image and likeness of God. If we were to work in fulfilling our own words whilst we are on this earth, we will be afflicted later because we have not recognized the mystery of His Words to us.

CHAPTER TWO

Believe You Can Succeed & You Will

BELIEVE YOU CAN SUCCEED & YOU WILL

***Mark. 11:23** "What You Say Is What You Get."*
"Do you see this mountain? If you want to move it, all you have to do is speak to it and if you believe what you say, then you can have it. You can have whatsoever you say."

What You Say Is What You Get. I have known this to be true. I have moved mountains in my own life, not actual ones; but I have had success that exceeded my own expectations and my own capabilities. Just think back when you have thought of something good and it automatically happened to you. You then put it down to a miracle or just luck. You said it, and it happened. When I was growing up, and in a position to start experiencing life, I truly felt that I was put on this earth to achieve something good for my life and people around me, maybe God was trying to minister to me? However, unfortunately I was too naive in listening. What I thought I knew was that I had this burning desire to achieve the impossible; to achieve something greater than what I originally thought I could. I wanted to be a trailblazer, an admiral in industry, to achieve goals and ambitions, to learn from my earthly father's experiences in life and to improve on his achievements. I always thought that I was not gifted with luck; I had to work hard for it. At that time in my life, I also believed in myself and that it was down to me in achieving any goals in life that I set. What I did believe in was God and Christ our Savior, with little understanding of God's Written Words in the Bible.

MY FIRST IMPRESSION OF LIFE

My first real impression of life and of people in this world was through my role model and mentor, my earthly father Michael, a man that to this day I looked up to. Through my years, I have molded a similar drive and determination to enjoy a pleasing life. The difference at the time between my father and I, was that Michael had an intimate relationship with God and not through lack of trying, my father was always saying to my brothers and I, turn for Gods help in everything you do.

"God looks down from heaven on the sons of men to see if there are any who understand, any who seek God." **(Psalm 53:2.)**

Whenever I needed to redirect my career or personal life, I would seek the help of my dad, who advised me to pray. God would listen to my prayer and give me a taste, a morsel; of what it life could really be like in having an intimate relationship with Him.

"I the Lord search the heart and examine the mind, to reward a man according to his conduct, according to what his deeds deserve." **(Jeremiah 17:10)**

"Is anyone of you in trouble? He should pray. Is anyone happy? Let him sing songs of praise." **(James 5:13.)**

I felt that success was my middle name and at the age of 16 years, I was running one of the most successful men's retail stores in the group. At 19 years, I started my first outside sales job, being the youngest in the company and during my first year with them, I was the number one executive out of over 90+ older salespeople. I was worth three salesman, with month after month, over sales target achievements for six years. I had always believed in helping people in business rather than manipulating them to buy. I also showed a true, genuine desire in serving my customers. The problem was; I would forget who gave me my success and did not really know why and for what purpose? After a period, I prayed frequently to God, not sure if he was listening. I was still thinking at this stage in my life, should I be reading his Word in the Bible. Every time that I tried to read the Bible, the pages seemed endless, with none of the words really making sense. A few years had passed and I felt it was important to meet a soul mate. I found myself a wife, a non-believer in God, which rubbed off onto me later in our relationship. Soon after, we started a family and shared our love with two wonderful sons. I felt that the world was my oyster. "Bring it on baby!" *"The way of a fool is right in his own eyes: but he that hearkeneth unto counsel is wise."* **(Proverbs 12:15.)**

By the age of 28, I felt that I needed to find true direction in my life as well as my career that was getting a bit stagnated. I remembered as a child, how I loved pretending to be a cowboy, riding on the back of my mother's sofa in my cowboy outfit, being totally enthralled by the cowboy films on TV. How I wished to be in America! I decided to seek God help for this change and prayed that He would widen my territories in foreign lands. I remember my dad having a dream one night, maybe a vision.

My dad (Michael) said; I was beside a man of wealth, who was shaking my hand; it seemed a very important meeting for me. "Not to say that my dad was a fortuneteller, or something like that!" He was concerned for me as you would, if you too dreamed about your child. He also told me that this man might have been talking about traveling somewhere overseas. A few months later, that dream came to life. I met a man who could see that I had an entrepreneur nature and wanted me to work for him, promoting furniture manufacturers to retailers, and guess where? You got it, America.

"Only be thou strong and very courageous, that thou mayest observe to do according to all the law, which Moses my servant commanded thee: turn not from it to the right hand or to the left, that thou mayest prosper whithersoever thou goest." **(Joshua 1:7.)**

On my first visit to America, the plane was experiencing landing problems due to a storm in Newark, New York. The captain of the airplane talked to us through a speaker, letting us know there would be a delay, but not to worry. Whilst he was talking I started to think that we would likely crash or run out of fuel in the air and then crash, the plan was going through the storm bumping and banging in turbulence. At this point, a positive thought came to me not to worry, thinking about it I was sure that God was communicating with me. I started to feel relaxed that everything would be fine and felt confident that the plane would land safely. When we finally landed and by the time, it took to go through immigration, it was getting extremely late.

My work colleges that were expecting me at least 4 hours previously, more then likely had left the tradeshow in Highpoint North Carolina, and I still needed to find were my connecting plane was in the airport. I also realized that all my colleges phone numbers were in my luggage bags that were around the airport somewhere and had no way of contacting them. I also could not remember what hotel or even the address of where I was staying. "What a nightmare." I started to walk swiftly through the airport most of the connecting flights to other states were being canceled due to the bad weather so I sat down in despair. I lifted my head and saw two elderly women approached me and they started up a conversation. These two women reminded me of my grandma, sweet, and kind, they even shared their cookies with me whilst we were awaiting news regarding their connecting flights. These two wonderful women told me that they lived close by and should I be stuck in the airport for the night, I could go home with them. "Bless their hearts." I told them that it was my first trip to America and my job responsibilities could not allow me to stay in Newark overnight. I asked them to look after my hand held luggage, so that I could find help. Fortunately, there was a commuter plane taking flight attendants to Greensboro, North Carolina. (That was the airport where I needed to land for the Highpoint tradeshow location.) The person on the desk told me it was about to leave and I would need to run and catch the flight, which was on the other side of the airport. I said to them that I had no idea were my main luggage was that was on the plan from England with me, they told me not to worry they will sort it out. So, I ran as fast as I could back to the two wonderful ladies and hugged them both, grabbed my walk on bag running as fast as possibly for this connecting flight. It seemed like I had run at full speed for at least a mile or more to the gate, I felt like passing out. They were just about to close the entranceway when I told them to stop. The sweat was pouring out of me and they could sense my distress.

Fortunately, I got on the plane and sat beside another man that was also able to get on this flight. I told him about my first taste of the USA and this plane experience. He told me that I must have a Guardian Angel with me to get on this final flight, that was just what I needed to hear and my faith soared to think God was with me. The plane took off and after a short period, we cleared the storm. When we landed in North Carolina around 2:00-3:00am, I stood by the luggage turntable thinking was this in vain? Will I be waiting here all day? How could they have possibly got my luggage on to this flight in time? Then to my surprise, there was the luggage. Thank you God and all involved at Continental. Fortunately, the rest of my business trip went well.

"*The Angel of the Lord encampeth round about them that feared Him and deliverreth them. O taste and see that the Lord is Good: Blessed in the man that trusteth in Him.*" **(Psalms 34: 7, 8.)**

After a number of years, I had made many promises to the Lord our God. Through all my successes, I started to become vain, arrogant, and proud of all my own achievements. My success was great as I constantly learning new trades in business within the country of my dreams and ambition. During my personal life, I stayed true to my wife although my job was keeping me at times away from home. God was slowly leaving my life, as I had forgotten Him whilst I was wrapped up in what I thought was my own success. Years later, things started to go wrong in my marital life as my wife found new interests and it was not me anymore, this had a dramatic affect on my career. I decided to seek the Lord's advice, but it was too late.

***Ezekiel** 7:9* *"I will not look on you with pity or spare you; I will repay you in accordance with your conduct and the detestable practice among you. Then you will know that it is I the Lord who strikes the blow."*

I felt that God had let me down; I could not believe it was happening to me. To say I was annoyed, hurt and offended was an understatement and I blamed God and Jesus for my failed marriage and business downfall. During one of my visits around America, I became extremely ill; I was rushed into hospital for a life threatening operation. I had a hole in my colon that created some form of poison puss ball in my stomach lining ready to explode and kill me. All the nurses were praying for me daily and one of the nurse's put an angel figurine in my room. I realized it was a sign for me to make my peace with God, by pleading for my life in Jesus name. After a tremendous ordeal with drainage pumps to get the infection out of me, I had further complications with blood clots in my legs and lungs. "Another life threatening ordeal." To cut this traumatic experience short, once I was stable they operated on me and after four week of bed rest as well as losing well over 60lbs in weight, I started to recover and flew back to England.

Psalm 41:2,3,4. *"The LORD will preserve him, and keep him alive; and he shall be blessed upon the earth: and thou wilt not deliver him unto the will of his enemies. The LORD will strengthen him upon the bed of languishing: thou wilt make all his bed in his sickness. I said, LORD, be merciful unto me: heal my soul; for I have sinned against thee."*

By the time I got back to England, I had lost my wife to another man yet again, I could no longer sleep in the same bed, let alone live with her in the same house, and my dearly beloved children were stopped from seeing me through her embarrassing behavior. I could no longer live the life that I made for myself. After a period a further 2 months recuperating with my loss and building strength from my operation, my employer at the time was trying to get me back into a work mode, mainly because they wanted further business expansions. I still needed at this point, a further month off work. Unfortunately, the company would not see my point of view as they felt it would be better for me to work, or potentially be replaced. A few days later, I had to attend a very important meeting; it was raining hard and extremely cold. I crawled out of bed, and got prepared for this meeting. I had to drive for three hours and realized I would be late, so I put my foot down hard to get there on time. One hour had past I was sweating heavily in my car seat; the rain was belting down, and I remember looking at the speed that the car was moving; I'd better slowdown from 109. Just then, the car started to aquaplane out of control, bouncing from one barrier to the other on this four-lane highway. There was absolutely nothing I could do to control the car, as I could also see the barriers that I was fastly approaching to crash in to with great force. As I hit the barriers I could see behind me the barriers buckle and bend, it looked like I had tore up at least 200 yards of barrier as I was bouncing from side, to side of the barriers. On the final bounce back from the left hand-side of the barrier, the car straightened going head-on towards the other side of the highway in the direction of the on coming traffic. "At this point, I felt my time had come." All of a sudden, everything went into slow motion; there was a glowing light in the car just as if the sun had shone into a bedroom with lightweight curtains against the window.

I remember a voice saying; turn the wheel, which I did calmly. The car then hit the barrier again and everything sped back up. Instead of me crashing through the barrier head on, the car hit it sideways on and bounced me back to the left side barrier of the highway. I came to a slow grinding stop. I sat there for what seemed like a minute, very calmly with no though going through my mind. I looked around and saw a truck driver who ran up to me and asked in a very loud voice; "are you I still alive mate?" I could not talk for a few seconds due to what may have been shock. I turned my head round to him and replied; "yes I think so." The truck driver could not believe that was still alive and ran back to his truck to get his steel crowbar to get me out. After a few minutes standing in the cold rain, I then picked up my cell phone and called my boss to tell him of the news. He first thing that he asked me was if the new car was OK. A week later, I resign from my position as vice-president of sales and marketing. That was my fourth life- threatening experience. During my sorrow and morning of losing everything that was once good in my life. I decided to pull myself back together, and looked at ways to re-launch my career by setting up a company of my own. Most of the time, it was short-term gains, due to poor company structure and my attitude to life. I had to work much harder than I ever had to before. I felt that the gifts and blessings that I once had in my life lost.

1 Kings 2:2,3. *"I am about to go the way of all the earth, he said. So be strong, show yourself a man, and observe what the Lord your God requires: Walk in his ways, and keep his decrees and commands, his laws and requirements, as written in the Law of Moses, so that you may prosper in all you do and wherever you go."*

I decided to gain a better understanding of God and his ways; I had tried to recharge my batteries only to find out that I needed new ones. I looked at all my training books, and listened to the motivational tapes. They just did not work. I then prayed for solutions and realized I did not need to look that far. God had forgiven me for my sins through my confessions. (I realized, He was the Creator.) He had written how to succeed in life. He was my mentor and trainer, with a force more tremendous, more powerful than I have ever experienced, in anyone or anything. He had already shown me signs of success. I realized, quickly, that I was now given yet another chance to start again, not to look back on my life's mistakes. God gave me chances to repent repeatedly. There was a chance to understand His Word, chance to give Him praise, chances to believe, and chances to follow in His guidance. Now, if this was a form of career or full- time job, I would have been dismissed, fired for not complying with my job description. I realized that with God, this does not happen, providing we realize our mistakes and look to resolve them.

"*Though thy beginning was small, yet thy latter end should greatly increase. "If you are pure and upright, even now he will rouse himself on your behalf and restore you to your rightful place. Your beginnings will seem humble, so prosperous will your future be."* **(Job 8:6,7.)**

During the next few weeks, I had found a new place to live, which was a lot smaller, and something that I was not used to living in. I sat in my chair, as that was the only thing at the time I had in this property. I sat there for at least 24 hours totally washed out. Whilst I was sitting there drowning in tears, I started praying begging Jesus to come in to my life.

I said to Jesus that I want to change and believe. I needed to restore my faith in God and continued to confessed my inadequacies, obligated the Lord to tell me what I needed to do. "Tell me Lord and I will do it?" I sat in my home for three days and nights. Jesus was my mediator; He will work hard for me, He will tell God that I have made my commitment to Him and this time for good. I remember thinking, at that time, what are you doing? Are you sure that you are not waiting for nothing? It is up to you. Come on Andrew, you can do it. You can do it again, you are a trailblazer; you are an admiral of industry. "Success has been written for you and rubber-stamped." Then reality kicked in. Jesus told me; "who are you trying to kid? Your own motivation doesn't last long enough." I jumped out of my chair and shouted believe, pray, go to church, get out of the house, do something. Therefore, I went out for a walk unshaven, still in the same clothes that I had been wearing since moving in to that shack of a home. I was walking in circles, clasping my hands like a mad man and closing my eyes, praying and praying very hard. "I know you are up there, I know you are listening. I know you can help me."

After the pacing and all of the praying, I had calmed down. When you pray, something good happens as all your burdens are relieved, you feel wonderful warmth inside, and that is indescribable. I went in the house, to make a cup of hot tea. I stood there watching the kettle, waiting for it to boil. Wow, it was taking a long time. After it had boiled, I poured the water into the teapot. Then, "Ping" I had a revelation. JESUS told me to go to America, I thought; "am I going mad". However, in my heart and my sole, I knew. "Don't ask me how." I was having a conversation with the Lord, and he said; "You are at your best in America, you have helped a lot of people in business over there. You have already helped a number of people turn failure into victory."

Jeremiah 29:11,12. *"For I know the plans I have for you, declares the Lord, plans to prosper you and not to harm you, plans to give you hope and a future. Then you will call upon me and come and pray to me, and I will listen to you."*

I realized for my life to be turned around again, this time for the good, I had to truly believe in Jesus and as that is what He communicated to me, would happen. To have confidence in Jesus, you have to believe in his faith. I also realized that manifestation could not happen if you do not have faith. When you obligate Jesus to find solutions to our prayer, you have to believe it will happen. When you obligate Jesus, he will then become obligated to see it through providing that it is what should be for your life. When you do not believe, it will not happen for what you have prayed." ***Mark. 11:24 "Believe that you have received."***

JESUS & THE CENTURION

Matthew.8: 5-13. This is the written word about a centurion that went to Jesus for him to heal his servant. The centurion knew of Jesus ability to heal people. He was also confident in knowing, that when Jesus was obligated by his people's requests, he had to see that the obligation was met for the right reasons. The centurion knew this because he worked for people with authority, and people that worked for him did what was asked.

"It Shall Be Done, Believe That You Have Received."

This centurion had faith in Jesus' ability based on his confidence of authority. ***5. And when Jesus was entered into Capernaum, there came unto him a centurion, beseeching him. 6. And saying, Lord, my servant lieth at home sick of the paisy, grievously tormented. 7. And Jesus saith unto him "I will come and heal him."*** (Now, nowhere in these scriptures does Jesus say; are you a Christian, do you go regular to church, are you a believer of my Father's Words?) ***8. The centurion answered and said. Lord, "I am not worthy that thou shouldest come under my roof: but speak the word only, and my servant shall be healed.9. For I am a man under authority, having soldiers under me: and I say to this man, Go, and he goeth: and to another, come and he cometh; and to my servant, do this, and he doeth it."10. When Jesus heard this he was marveled, and said unto him "I have not found so great faith, no, not in Israel. Go thy way; and as thou hast believed, so it shall be done."***

What I loved to read was the following scripture in the Bible: For Jesus was marveled, he could not believe that this centurion understood how God structures worked. (I found that incredible.) Here is a man that obligated Jesus through belief. The centurion could have easily not believed from being; negative, or having fear. The centurion probably felt that his job was a little like Jesus'. I am asked to do something and I do it. He was obligated by his leaders' words to make sure that they are followed through, completed, and achieved. His superiors trusted the centurion that they to had faith in him completing any multiply, or single tasks, no matter the level of difficulty. (Isn't that amazing?) Continuing my life story, I felt that Jesus was asking me to contact a man in America. This man owned a company that was marketing furniture and struggling for sales. We originally met at one of the largest international trade shows in America. The last time I was exhibiting furniture products at this trade show, this man was also there. I remembered seeing him out of the corner of my eye. He was pacing up and down next to my showroom area, he could see that I was busy, so he kept pacing up and down of the walkway desperate to talk. Towards the end of the show, he was trying to grab my attention; I was having a successful show in making money for my company. Finally, he said to the person next to me; "Can you tell him that I need to talk with him urgently." This was the last day of the show, and it was a panic in getting packed up and flying back to England. My conscious told me to go see him, more than likely God was playing a part. I went up and met him. He showed me a fantastic range of imported furniture and told me that he had invested all his money into this furniture line, needing to make good profit before it bankrupted him. To cut this story short, when I got my revelation; I was obliged to see this through. I phoned him and organized a visit. By this time, he was getting ready to cut his own throat.

When I arrived in America, he could not thank me enough and said; "I will give you a share in the company, I will pay you well, what do you want?" I was in a position to tie him down; he needed help badly. The rarity of his products was limited; this meant that any of this furniture being manufactured, had a limited supply with top dollar pricing. I could have taken advantage, but I did not. I said to him; "I really don't know? Let us see how it goes. You pay me what you feel is suitable, but do me a favor, do not promise what you cannot later deliver." I answered him this way because I was still unsure of what my purpose in helping he would be. I was not going to offend anyone, you know whom! After the trade-show, where we gained success in selling to various retailers, he asked me to go back home with him, to continue marketing his company's product. At this point, I needed to decide whether to leave everything behind in England, my children whom were still with their mother, my parents and brothers, including many unfinished problems in my life. I thought at the time I was getting the raw deal, the short straw, but I knew that I needed to be obedient to God and had to see this through with no doubts.

Genesis 12:1. ***"The Lord said to Abram, "Leave your country, your people and your father's household and go to the land I will show you."***

Leaving the tradeshow behind us, we had driving for least 6 hours, when he grabbed a bottle of wine from under his seat. I sat there quiet whilst he was drinking. I said; "Would you like me to drive as it's a bad idea to drink, whilst you are driving?" He said; "I have done this hundreds of times before, it is a straight road for hundreds of miles, chill-out." I looked out of the window and thought what am I doing here.

Eight hours later and with a drunk driver, I was listening to a radio station that said we were driving directly into a major storm that could become a hurricane. I could not believe what was happening, it was something that would have been shown in a movie. We were driving all night long and in the early hours of the morning, we had finally made it to his house, were his wife and family were waiting for us. Within a few days, I had found out he was a manic depressant and already knowing he was an alcoholic. I prayed again for a miracle to get me out of this situation. The problem was they had the look in their eyes of desperation, needing my help and support. I felt like running away, back to England, but knew I had to see this through. I felt that I was at a junction, or roadblock, that had to be moved and knowing that this was something, I could not just simply move around.

CHAPTER THREE

Spiritual Roadblocks

JONAH'S ROADBLOCK

There will come a time in your life, when you cannot seem to do right for wrong, everything around you falls apart, and you are looking for solutions. Thoughts go through your mind and you wonder what you can do to better your situation. The majority of your positive thoughts are from God, who is trying to show you the best way forward. Sometimes, even our Lord will put roadblocks in your way to bring you back onto the straight path of success. When God feels that He needs to pull you closer towards Him, you must listen for his words and His mentoring. Roadblocks kept coming up against me. I realized that God wanted me to be patient and wait. I felt that trying to open the doors, myself would lead me into being disobedient, and I needed to wait for doors to be opened by God. When I talk about waiting for doors to be opened, I am not talking about sitting around waiting until you receive a sign, like a bolt of lighting. What you have to do is reevaluate what is going on in your life, and pray for solutions. God will minister to you and this will be expressed through your mind and heart. Even other people/strangers, will start to come on your problems that have been instructed by God to assist you. When you are desperate, it is far easier to rush around like a headless chicken, and do something that will result in temporary happiness. If you feel God is ministering to you, it is best not to run away from Him. In the Bible, Jonah experienced major roadblocks in his life. "As I am sure we all have had at one time or another." In my younger years, I found this story a little bit hard to believe, especially when they talk about a whale swallowing up Jonah then spitting him out, still being alive. Then I thought, as I truly believe that God created everything the heavens and the earth, our fleshly bodies, why could He not create a whale to swallow up Jonah.

This scripture became realistic to me, whilst I was helping these people run their business. I was aware that God put me here for a purpose and it would have been easy to be disobedient, by running away from my responsibility of assisting them. My other though was that there could be another reason that God has put me here and not just to help them. I needed therefore to wait with anticipation, as the plan was being to unfold. To get a better understanding of what I was experiencing, let us look at the scriptures in the Bible regarding Jonah. This scripture began when the word of the Lord came to Jonah. ***"Go to the great city of Nineveh and preach against it, because its wickedness has come up before me."*** However, Jonah ran away from the Lord heading in a different direction. He decided to pay a fare, and sailed for Tarshish to flee from the Lord. God sent a spiritual roadblock in the way of a storm; it was such a violent storm that it threatened to break up the ship. All the sailors on board of the ship were afraid, and each cried out to their false gods, at this time Jonah had gone below deck where he was fast asleep. (I know a number of people that when they are completely stressed all they want to do is sleep to forget their responsibilities.) The captain went to him and said, ***"How can you sleep? Get up and call on your God! Maybe he will take notice of us, and we shall not perish."*** **Then the sailors said to each other,** ***"come, let us cast lots/draw straws to find out who is responsible for this storm."*** They cast lots and the lot fell on Jonah. Therefore, they asked him: ***"Tell us, who is responsible for making all this trouble for us? What do you do? Where do you come from? What is your country? From what people are you?"*** He answered, ***"I am a Hebrew and I worship the Lord, the God of heaven, who made the sea and the land."*** This terrified them and they asked; ***"What have you done?"*** (They automatically knew he was running away from the Lord, because they could sense it.) Jonah knew that if he stayed on board of the ship all the sailors would die from the storm, so he asked the crew members to throw him overboard, so that they would be saved.

The sailors decided to try and row the ship back to shore instead of throwing Jonah overboard, but the storm was getting worse. They cried to Jonahs' God and asked for forgiveness before they threw him into the sea. (In the Bible, it showed that the sailors made vows to God and converted their religion over to Him. It is just simply amazing how powerful our God can always be.) The storm then stopped and the sea became calm. God then sent another spiritual roadblock and summoned a whale to swallow up Jonah. While he was dying, Jonah prayed to God for deliverance from death. Jonah thought himself as good as dead, but the Lord heard his prayer and spared his life. Jonah then continued to seek Gods Will and did what God had asked him for his life. Believers should never give up hope in seemingly impossible situations. Jonah knew he had been disobedient, and recognized that it was God who threw him into the sea. When we pray, we must believe that our prayers go to Gods very presence in heaven, and that our Lord will intervene on our behalf. Continuing my testimonial, I realized that I still had a lot to accomplish; I could see that this man was slowly going crazy, as he was on some very heavy medication that he refused to take. He was close to losing everything, including his million-dollar home. In this man's earlier life, he had written a book of poems that illustrated his dislike for God by also stating that he was god; I had to sit with him in sharing the passages in this book. I thought to myself: "I'm in the house of hell." I am sure that his wife had having similar feelings, as I could see it in her eyes. The following morning, I put together goals and strategies to enable us in succeeding. I asked Jesus to intervene for me, to get out of this situation in helping this family.

One evening his wife sat down with me and explained about all of her problems, including her marriage to her husband. Not knowing them for very long, I tried to give her the best advice, telling her she needed to pray about the situation and maybe go to church. Sure enough, the following Sunday off she went to church.

Business started to pick-up "thank God" and we landed a number of lucrative orders. My relationship with him was getting a little bit better and his wife appeared to find more strength in herself. We had an opportunity of landing a large order, as I needed to visit the buyer in North Carolina. This man said to me that it was important for us both to go. Whilst we were driving to our appointment, he stated how important his family was to him and this project. He explaining how this order would give him the success needed to improve his relationship with his wife and children. When we arrived at our destination, we sat inside the car working out objectives for the meeting. He said; "Can you think of anything else?" I replied; "Let us hope God is with us today and it would help for us to pray." Sure enough, he closed his eyes and started to pray. I could not believe what I was seeing and I prayed silently with him. It was a very moving experience. Both of us jumped out of the car, and went through the main entrance, needless to say the meeting went extremely well.

1 Chronicles 16:10,11,12. *"Glory in his holy name, let the hearts of those who seek the Lord rejoice. Look to the Lord and his strength; seek his face always. Remember the wonders he has done, his miracles, and the judgments he pronounced."*

I felt God's Spirit move within me in helping this family, whether it was to get them out of a financial mess. On the other hand, to sow the seed of faith and belief, or maybe a test for me from God? To this end, do you know who, or what is the Holy Spirit? The Holy Spirit is a real person who came to reside within the true followers of Jesus, after He rose from the dead and ascended to heaven **(Read Acts 2).**

Jesus told His apostles... ***"I will ask the Father, and He will give you another Helper, that He may be with you forever; the Spirit of truth, whom the world cannot receive, because it does not behold Him or know Him, but you know Him because He abides with you, and will be in you. I will not leave you as orphans; I will come to you."*** **(John 14:16-18)**

THE HOLY SPIRIT

The Holy Spirit is not a vague, ethereal shadow, nor an impersonal force. He is a person equal in every way with God the Father and God the Son. He is considered the third member of the Godhead. Jesus said to His apostles... *"All authority has been given to Me in heaven and on earth. Go therefore and make disciples of all the nations, baptizing them in the name of the Father and the Son and the Holy Spirit, teaching them to observe all that I commanded you; and lo, I am with you always, even to the end of the age."* **(Matt. 28:18-20)**

God is Father, Son and Holy Spirit, with all the divine attributes ascribed to the Father and the Son being equally ascribed to the Holy Spirit. When a person becomes born again by believing and receiving Jesus Christ **(John 1:12-13; John 3:3-21)**, God resides in that person through the Holy Spirit **(1Cor. 3:16)**.

The Holy Spirit has intellect **(1Cor. 2:11)**, emotion **(Romans. 15:30)**, and will **(1Cor. 12:11)**. A primary role of the Holy Spirit is that He bears "witness" of Jesus Christ **(John 15:26, 16:14)**. He tells people's hearts about the truth of Jesus Christ. The Holy Spirit also acts as a Christian's teacher **(1Cor. 2:9-14)**. He reveals God's will and God's truth to a Christian. Jesus told His disciples... *"The Helper, the Holy Spirit, whom the Father will send in My name, He will teach you all things, and bring to your remembrance all that I said to you."* **(John 14:26)** *"When He, the Spirit of truth, comes, He will guide you into all the truth; for He will not speak on His own initiative, but whatever He hears, He will speak; and He will disclose to you what is to come."* **(John 16:13)**

The Holy Spirit was given to live inside those who believe in Jesus, in order to produce God's character in the life of a believer. In a way that we cannot do on our own, the Holy Spirit will build into our lives love, joy, peace, patience, kindness, goodness, faithfulness, gentleness, and self-control. **(Gal. 5:22-23)**.

Rather than us trying to be loving, patient, kind, as God asks us to rely on Him to produce these qualities in our lives. Thus, Christians are told to walk in the Spirit **(Gal. 5:25)** and be filled with the Spirit **(Eph. 5:18)**. The Holy Spirit empowers Christians to perform ministerial duties that promote spiritual growth among Christians **(Romans. 12; 1Cor. 12; pH. 4).**

The Holy Spirit also performs a function for non-Christians as well as He convicts peoples hearts about the truth of God and how sinful we can be whereby we need to seek forgiveness from God. The Holy Spirit also tells us on how righteous Jesus is and how He died in our place, for our sins and God's eventual judgment of the world and those who do not know Him **(John 16:8-11)**. The Holy Spirit tugs on our hearts and minds, asking us to repent and turn to God for forgiveness for a new life.

FINDING AN ANGEL

Back to my testimonial: After five months marketing these furniture products, we were in a position to part and for me to move on into other ventures with God. I was feeling lonely in my life, with nobody to share my true thoughts or feelings with and felt it was time for me to move on. However, if I went back to England, there would be no partner for me to wrap my arms around to feel comfort and security. My ex-wife, through hard feelings, would only let me speak to my boys by phone and financially, I gave every penny to her for the children, including the home that we shared together. There was a company in England at that time I felt would employ me. Should I stay or stray and go back to England? I prayed that God would intervene in this situation, to enable all of our lives to move on positively. The following week I decided to visit a few historical places in Charleston and drove there not really knowing were to start my evening. Whilst I got lost walking around downtown Charleston, I saw this beautiful young woman and knew straight away in my mind and spirit that I needed to know her more. I knew under the circumstance of me being in this place at that moment in time was no accident of being lost and felt that it was a start of God's new plan for my life. There was no other conceivable way, even by chance of me meeting her like this and knew that fate is no longer a word in my life. God also made me to forget were I had parked my car, so that Angela would have to drive me home. I am sure this was to build more of a personal relationship with her and her with me. Least to say we left downtown Charleston together and before being dropped off at my temporary residence, we walked the Beach on the Isle of Palms for hours upon end, simply talking to each other.

Proverbs 18:22 *"He that finds a wife finds what is good and receives favor from the Lord."*

After many months of seeing each, I took her back to England in the hope of talking her into staying there with me and at the same time whilst I was sorting a number of personal issues out. In the end, Angela decided that she did not want to be away from her parents and asked me to live in America with her in continuing our relationship. This was a mutual feeling, as I felt God was blessing us both in being together. When we got back, to America we went to church and the pastor was happy to share in our marriage arrangements. This time it felt so right for us both to be together as Angela was a believer in God's plan for her life. I had absolutely nothing to offer her in the way of financial stability as I was awaiting approval for a green card to work in America. Angela said: "I will provide for both of us, until you find what God has intended for you to do. I had never met a human being like this before outside of God and or my own family that had ever offered so much commitment, loyalty, and faith.

Matthew 25:35,36 "*For I was hungry and you gave me something to eat, I was thirsty and you gave me something to drink, I was a stranger and you invited me in, I needed clothes and you clothed me, I was sick and you looked after me.*"

I was feeling extremely guilty, as I had always been very successful in life and used to being the only financial provider. Angela (my Angel) was also praying and looking for a long time for a person that she too could love and build a life with that had the same belief as a Christian. Angela was now taking me to a higher level with God.

TALKING TO JESUS

Whilst I was figuring out what to do in my life, I became a little despondent; I also had many negative thoughts. That night whilst I was praying and praising our Lord through confessing my inadequacies, I then decided to talk to Jesus in prayer to provide solutions for me in my new life here in America. ***Joshua 1:7,8.*** *"Be strong and very courageous. Be careful to obey all the law my servant Moses gave you; do not turn from it to the right or the left, that you may be successful wherever you go. Do not let this Book of Law depart from your mouth; meditate on it day and night, so that you may be careful to do everything written in it. Then you will be prosperous and successful."*

The following morning, I jumped into the car driving towards the highway. I was in a subconscious state not very sure of what I needed to do, or where I was going. Normally, I would worked out were I wanted to go and studied a map to get the exact directions. I had a warm but secure feeling within me that something was going to happen. I had faith and trust in Jesus seeing out the obligation that I gave him. Sure enough, I saw a company sign; I did not bother questioning why I felt the urge in seeing them. "I just went with the flow." When I got to this company, they were holding interviews for sales positions. I thought to myself, " Let me see what happens." I asked if I could see the general manager. The receptionist said that he was interviewing; I was persistent enough to wait until he had finished. While I was waiting, a man walked through the door; he was there for a 1pm interview. When the general manager came out to greet who he thought was his next applicant, he had a confused look on his face.

There were two of us. So I introduced myself to him and stated, "I have come to make your day more interesting than it already is." Needless to say, within the following hour, I was sitting in front of the general manager being interviewed. I knew that he was going to offer me the job, even before I had spoken to him. Sure enough at the end of the interview, he said. "Why should I offer you this position?" I replied, "I have prayed about it. I have been sent here; and have been told that you will offer me one of your vacancies." I could not believe that I said that to him; it just came out of my mouth. There was an automatic silence. I was thinking about the smart closing techniques that I have used in the past to win jobs. I was ready to kick myself when he said, "OK, when can you start?" Now if that is not obligating Jesus I do not know what is. Sure enough, like Jesus said to the centurion, "Go thy way; and thou hast believed, and so be it done unto thee." What a Revelation! Now, there was a catch. Jesus, in return for answering me, threw a challenge straight back. After the general manager offered me the position, he told me that there were a number of his employees that were uneducated, drank, and swore heavily, they also had no respect for management and defiantly not for sales people. That was my next challenge and as time went on, I proved to be their top sales person and earned respect and trust from their disgruntled employees, which I still have as good friends. Do you realize that all of us posses spiritual gifts? These are tools given unto us for faith, obedience, and belief. They are the most powerful tools we could ever posses. With spiritual gifts, you can have supernatural motivation, a motivation that comes from your spiritual inside of you through God and not your own self-motivation. Like anything in life, it comes from having total faith in God. So how can we build a structure around us that will help us to God's blessings of these spiritual gifts? Well, it starts by praying, repenting of your sins, believing in God and having faith that Jesus died on the cross for our sins.

DREAMING OF JESUS

Whilst I was studying Gods Words, my thoughts started turning to Jesus. I realized that over the years God had played a very big role in my life and I had grown in true belief and love for God, But what about Jesus? I felt that maybe I do not have the same relationship with Jesus, as I have with God. I knew that I felt the three parts of God. (The Father, Son & Holy Spirit.) However, what about Jesus? I am very embarrassed to state this; but did I truly feel the same way in Jesus, have the same faith and love as I could express in my heart, as I do for God? Do I feel that Jesus is a member of my family, as you would love a brother, sister, mother, father and more? I truly felt a total fraud to God. How could I conceivably consider the mere thought, that Jesus did not have the same love and respect that exist in my heart and if this was the case, am I truly saved as a believer? That night, I went to bed very confused and upset, as I realized that I must have had uncertainty about His existence. That very night, Jesus came to me in a vision. I was standing at an altar with my wife, Angela. We were both looking at each other smiling; I was thinking that my life felt complete. Jesus came into the room in a majestic way. As he approached the pulpit, Jesus pointed to a large Bible with old discolored pages. Jesus was then flipping the pages from left to right, He was pointing to specific scriptures. As I was looking to were Jesus was pointing, all I could read was blessed are those? Blessed is he? Blessed is the man? Blessed are thee? Angela's body language confirmed understanding of these scriptures, while I was overwhelmed by Jesus' presence with us. I tried to show my understanding of the scriptures; but could only read the first few sentences of what He was showing to us both. As I turned around to look at Angela, she was walking away from me, smiling and waving in a loving way.

As I looked at Jesus, He pointed to a word that I had no understanding of **"Tribulation."** He then told me we needed to leave together. I remember asking the Lord; where are we going? From what I remember, Jesus replied: I need you to do something? Follow me. At that point, I awoke from my dream as Angela walked into the room and asked me if I slept well. I told her about the dream. During that day, I grabbed the Bibles we had around the house to try to find the scriptures that Jesus had pointed to. I could not remember what part of the Bible Jesus was relating to, but remembered the first few verses of the scriptures. I also recalled approximately were these verses were in relation to each page, whether it was top right, bottom right, and middle left of the pages. As I turned the pages of our Bibles, these scriptures did not relate to the page positions. I was becoming very frustrated and prayed that Jesus would reveal the Word of God to me again. I asked for forgiveness for not truly understanding what He was showing me in my dream. A few hours later, a voice came within me and said: "Go into the attic of your home." At this point, I had no intention to go up in the attic, but felt obligated in doing this. As I climbed the ladder into the attic, I was wondering what the purpose was for doing this. As I stood there looking around at all the items that had been stored in the past by Angela well before I had met her, I realized that it was the first time that I had ever gone into this attic. I said; what am I looking for? (In a displeasing manner.) Jesus said, "Look to your right". As I did what Jesus told me, I saw a brown paper package tied with string. I picked it up and went downstairs to where Angela was. I asked her, what is this? Angela said that it was a present from her Grandma, a family Bible. She then told me that her former roommate Shelby had wrapped it up and placed it in the attic. Angela had forgotten all about this Bible. I started unwrapping the Bible and as I turned the cover, to my surprise, were the yellow discolored pages.

As I started turning more of the pages, my hands started shaking with nervousness; I instinctively found the scriptures that Jesus showed me, in the exact same place of this Bible. The Bible was King James Version "Our Family Bible" Nelson Regency 702WM. That was the first time in my life that I truly cried tears of joy with total relief. "What an experience". The following Psalms are what I feel Jesus was instructing me to learn from:

Psalm 128 - Blessed is everyone that feareth the Lord that walketh in His ways... This Psalm related to fearing the Lord our God that is normally an overlooked element of worship, it also teaches to walk in His Words and ways so that we may be blessed.

Psalm 119 - Blessed are the undefiled in the way of the Lord Blessed are they that keep His testimonies... This Psalm is one of my favorites in the way it teaches us how to be happy (blessed) in doing the will of God in His Word. It teaches and talks about Gods Law, Commandments, Testimonies, Statues, Precepts, Judgments, Word, and Way. This skillfully written Psalm, so I understand, is written start to finish in the Hebrew Alphabet with each paragraph representing a Hebrew Letter alphabetically? This Psalm teaches us that we will grow in grace and righteousness only as love for the Word grows in us.

Psalm 112 - Praise ye the Lord Blessed is the man that feareth the Lord.... This Psalm speaks of the blessing in store for a God fearing and righteous person. God promises to bless those that fear Him and find delight in His commandments and written word.

Psalm 65 - Blessed is the man whom thou choseth and causeth to approach unto thee... I feel Jesus here was showing me that our greatest joy is to be near God and to enjoy communion with him; this is now possible for all believers through the sacrifice of Jesus Christ. The Bible exhorts us to draw near to God continually, that we might receive His mercy and strength to help us in our times of hardship.

Psalms 32 - Blessed is he whose transgressions is forgiven... This Psalm teaches us the only truly happy people are those who have received forgiveness of their sins from God and that their sins do not weigh heavily on their hearts. Confessing your sins to God honestly and sincerely always results in Gods gracious pardon. In this, Psalm God promises to instruct and guide a forgiven believer who has a teachable spirit.

This follow Psalm I feel was another one that Jesus was trying to show me, but I am not certain. Saying that it is a great Psalm to learn from:

Psalms 1 - Blessed is the man that walketh not in the council of the ungodly... This Psalm serves as an introduction on two types of people recognized by God. (1). The Godly, who are characterized by righteousness, love, obedience to God's Word. The ungodly, who represent the way of this world and who do not abide in Gods Word and who do not have no part in the assembly of Gods people. The end of this Psalm tells us to take refuge in God Almighty before the Day of Judgment arrives.

Next, I needed to find out the meaning of Tribulation, as this word is briefly shown in the Bible, it does not have a lot of information relevant to the word. It is more of a descriptive word; if I am not mistaken, it is in Revelations.

What Is The Tribulation?

The word "tribulation," used as a prophetic term, comes from Jesus' Olivet discourse, during which He laid out the future course of human history all the way to its climax at His Second Coming. The Lord said, in response to His disciples' question, "What shall be the sign of thy coming, and of the end of the world?"

"For then shall be great tribulation, such as was not since the beginning of the world to this time, no, nor ever shall be" **(Matthew 24: 21).**

"Tribulation" is the term for the general era of God's judgment on a rebellious world of earth-dwellers. It is a time, which will begin with Antichrist signing a seven-year covenant guaranteeing Israel's peace and security **(Daniel 9: 27)**.

This era is kicked off, symbolically, beginning with the first horseman of the Apocalypse **(Revelation 6: 1)**.

"Great Tribulation" is considered to be the last three and one-half years of that seven-year period known as "Daniel's seventieth week." The last three and one-half years is called "the time of Jacob's trouble" in Jeremiah 30: 7, when God's most horrific, but totally righteous wrath is poured directly upon the rebels of planet Earth. These judgments are portrayed and precisely outlined in Revelation, chapters 6 through 19. The Tribulation will end when Christ returns from Heaven to defeat God's enemies and set up His Millennial Kingdom on earth **(Revelation 19: 11-16)**.

During the tribulation, what will make-up the one world church? All people who have not given their lives to Jesus Christ will be a part of the one-world church. They will be deceived into worshiping the Antichrist until it is too late to turn back. These people will think that they are worshiping the Messiah and will do so gladly and blindly because they did not know the true Messiah. Unfortunately, many of these people will have called themselves Christians.

Do you know the true Messiah as your personal Savior and Lord? Do you know Him intimately? Would you recognize a slick impostor? If you have any doubt, then your salvation is in question. Ask the Lord to reveal Himself to you and to draw you unto Him. Ask Him to forgive your sins, especially the pride that has kept you from surrendering to Him until now.

CHAPTER FOUR

Structure For Success

FAITH, BELIEF & OBEDIENCE

I have always had a desire to help people in business, for the hope that they will receive some form of improvement in their life. When I pray, I look for solutions, not wealth, and success. I have always tried not to think about how much I will be earning, because God has always shown me the way in earning what I have needed. This has comes naturally for me out of belief and faith, in Gods ethical ways of life. Before I understood the Words of God, I used to look at my star sign, aquarius. There was always a downside in reading the daily star signs in magazines and or newspapers. When it stated, I was going to have a bad day, sure enough I did. I needed something that would always be positive and reassuring. When selling, I would imagine jumping in to the other person's shoes. I pictured myself as that buyer, his business, and/or that person, who needs help. "How can I truly give them what they really need to benefit there needs and for other around them?" Sure enough, God gave me the best solutions. If everyone could find their faith in the Lord, to read His words in the bible, to be obedient and have belief through faith, then Christianity within the workplace could easily work hand-in-hand. The problem is, too many keep straddling the fence of barbed wire and when they stumble "ouch" that hurts. When you can walk in the Words of God, and know God is mentoring to you, He will show favor. I would love to run an opinion poll throughout the world, for people the Lord our God helps and whether they knew it or not. You would be amazed at the millions or billions of people that are healed and have in many ways been rewarded for their faith, obedience, and belief. God is fully knowing that it takes time to become a true follower in His Word, as there is a lot to learn from all of His scriptures.

God has put His spirit in our body, and does not want us to live our lives in the flesh, but to detach ourselves from the worldly lives that we so desperately cling too.

Genesis.27: 8 *"Obey my voice to the commandments, the words of my voice."*

God has made you not to suffer life's experiences, but to excel in everything you achieve to do, you cannot command success, as God will give this to you and should you work for ungrateful people, concern yourself not. God is on your side and the longer you have to wait for your reward, the bigger shall the reward be in Heaven. There has only been God, who has never lost faith in you, who created you as a miracle and with miracles, they can never be improved on. God gave you the power to speak, to love, to succeed, to help others, to overcome fear, to be joyful, to be brave, to be strong, to create and to plan a purpose in life. Whilst we are discussing God's rewards I just thought about a person that I once knew that received a reward from God and I would like to share this testimonial with you. As a matter of interest, do you believe in Heaven? At one time in my life, when I was only 11 years old, I wondered about Heaven and how God rewards us, providing we live a life according to God's plan. I also wondered that if we strayed, or did not believe in the Lord Jesus, would we go to hell?

HEAVEN & MR. JACK BEAN

When I was 11 years old, we lived in a town called Hythe in Kent, which is in the South of England and for some unknown reason Kent, has always been classed as the earth's version of the Garden of Eden. My dad (Michael) purchased a large home called the Paddocks and in the early 18th century this home was owned by a very wealthy person, maybe a gentry or noble man of that period. The name "Paddock" was due to the fact that the owners, of that time, had stables and thoroughbred horses. During the Second World War, this home became a hospital for the wounded servicemen. By the time, my father purchased this property; it was extremely run down and in desperate need of repair. The main reason my father purchased this old home was to restore the property by making it a bed and breakfast motel, for tourist visiting Kent. The first priority was to turn the old stables in to a single story home and once that was completed, our family moved in. The main building consisted of 26 bedrooms with a living room, which would become the dining area; the formal living room would be a casual sitting room and in the back area of this home would be a large kitchen for preparing meals. There were many other rooms, which at some point would be converted in to some form of entertainment areas. When we moved in to the home my father told us about a few tenants already living there and they had what was called "squatters rights." In other words, they were in their rights to stay legally. Most of them said they would move out once they found suitable accommodation, but one old man was insistent that he stayed in his one bedroom, sectioned in the attic. My dad is a very obliging and kind man, telling them that it would be fine, but when the home was completely refurbished, they would then have to find suitable accommodation, and or stay providing they contributed towards a monthly rental.

This home demanded that as a family we would all help clear and clean out rooms so that my father could start his renovation work. I was given the formal dining area to work on and as I started the work, I could hear music playing somewhere in this home. I decided to go and investigate. As I followed the music, I started to climb the stairs up towards the attic and it was getting darker and darker the higher up the stairs that I went. I finally reached the top and was very nervous, I could see that there was a door slightly opened, and I could hear this old man muttering to himself. I then turned around and was about to run down the stairs as fast as my feet would take me, when he shouted; "hold your horses boy, come here." I stopped and turned around to this old man, he looked as black as a coal miner. This man looked as if he last took a bath maybe 10 or more years ago. He said; "don't worry boy, I do not bite and will not hurt you, come in for a minute." I did not really want to go in and my mother always told me, not to talk with stranger, unfortunately I was very inquisitive and decided go to him. Whilst I was in his room, it too was filthy dirty. He was living off a small oil type of stove that he cooked with and used it for light when it drew dark. The oil off this stove had turned the room black over the years. We talked for a while and he introduced himself as Mr. Jack Bean. During the next year, from time to time, I would see him and talk briefly with him. This one evening I saw him talking to a man and as he was talking, Mr. Bean was coughing very harshly; I went over to him and asked if he needed anything. Mr. Bean asked me to visit the pharmacist to get him medication. During that evening, after I had given Mr. Bean his medication, I told my mother that he was very sick and she said that once her daily chores were completed the next morning, she would go and check on him. Later I went to bed and fell a sleep and during that night, I had a dream. I remember that I was sitting on freshly cut grass in a playing field next to a path, as I sat their I saw mist starting to cover the ground and in the distance was a human figure running through the mist.

I was sitting there wondering, who is this person? As the person started to get closer, I realized that it was no other then Mr. Jack Bean. As he drew closer I noticed he was buck-naked and his skin was as white as white could be. I was thinking to myself, what is going on and as I was very embarrassed that he was naked. The other thing going through my mind was for an old man of mid to late sixties, he could run well and looked extremely healthy. As he passed me sitting on the grass, I noticed that he was smiling from ear to ear and waving at me. As he ran in the distance Mr. Bean was still waving. I awoke from the dream and during that morning after breakfast, my father asked me to start sweeping the floors in the dining area. I tried to make excuses for not wanting to do it but there was no getting out from my work. Whilst I was sweeping the floors, I did not hear any music from Mr. Bean's room, it was very unusual as I could always hear him playing his music from the room that I was working in. I decided to see if he was better, although I was feeling very strange about the dream that I had. For some unknown reason I feel that I had to see if, he was OK. As I went up the stairs, His door was slightly open, and I knocked on the door, there was no answer. I decided to stick my head around the door and look in to the room. To my surprise, Mr. Bean was naked dead on his bed; his body was still extremely dirty, as he had not taken a bath.

Over the years, a number of questions have come to mind, why did I have that dream of seeing him as a healthy, fit, **clean** and happy man. Where was he going? Why did he visit me in a dream or vision? There are still a few questions that puzzle me, to this day. Although I feel that he wanted to tell me goodbye and that, he was well again. I feel that he was on his way to heaven, mainly because I could sense his wonderful spirit whilst he was running, waving and smiling so happily.

So that leads on to my next question, what is heaven like, and what does the Bible say about heaven? I realize that it would be close to impossible to know exactly what heaven is truly like until we reach that point when our life end's. The Bible gives us a few clues and taste of what it could be like. Heaven is a place for the saved; there will be no God rejecter in heaven. I also believe that heaven will be so great and glorious that our minds cannot contain the blessings and riches of heaven. I am sure that for most people, that heaven probably has not crossed their minds before about the good things, God has prepared for His people in heaven.

"But as it is written, Eye hath not seen, nor ear heard, neither have entered into the heart of man, the things which God hath prepared for them that love him." **(1 Corinthians 2:9)**

Heaven will be so glorious that I am hard pressed to fully describe it. However, the Word of God does have some clues and even a brief description of heaven:

Heaven Is A Place Of Rewards - *"Rejoice, and be exceeding glad: for great is your reward in heaven: for so persecuted they the prophets which were before you."*

(Matthew 5:12) *"Rejoice ye in that day, and leap for joy: for, behold, your reward is great in heaven: for in the like manner did their fathers unto the prophets."* **(Luke 6:23)**

Heaven Is A Place Where God Is Worshiped - *"And the four beasts had each of them six wings about [him]; and [they were] full of eyes within: and they rest not day and night, saying, Holy, holy, holy, Lord God Almighty, which was, and is, and is to come. And when those beasts give glory and honor and thanks to him that sat on the throne, who liveth for ever and ever, The four and twenty elders fall down before him that sat on the throne, and worship him that liveth for ever and ever, and cast their crowns before the throne, saying, Thou art worthy, O Lord, to receive glory and honour and power: for thou hast created all things, and for thy pleasure they are and were created."* **(Revelation 4:8-11)**

Heaven Is A Place Where God Lives - *"Look down from thy holy habitation, from heaven, and bless thy people Israel, and the land which thou hast given us, as thou swarest unto our fathers, a land that floweth with milk and honey."* **(Deuteronomy 26:15)**

"Whosoever therefore shall confess me before men, him will I confess also before my Father which is in heaven. But whosoever shall deny me before men, him will I also deny before my Father which is in heaven." **(Matthew 10:32,33)**

Heaven Is A Place Of Tremendous Joy - *"Again, the kingdom of heaven is like unto treasure hid in a field; the which when a man hath found, he hideth, and for joy thereof goeth and selleth all that he hath, and buyeth that field."* **(Matthew 13:44)**

Treasures May Be Stored In Heaven - *"Then Jesus beholding him loved him, and said unto him, One thing thou lackest: go thy way, sell whatsoever thou hast, and give to the poor, and thou shalt have treasure in heaven: and come, take up the cross, and follow me."* **(Mark 10:21)**

Names Of The Saved Are Written In Heaven - *Notwithstanding in this rejoice not, that the spirits are subject unto you; but rather rejoice, because your names are written in heaven."* **(Luke 10:20)**

There Is No Sadness In Heaven - *"And God shall wipe away all tears from their eyes; and there shall be no more death, neither sorrow, nor crying, neither shall there be any more pain: for the former things are passed away."* **(Revelation 21:4)**

1. *"And I saw a new heaven and a new earth: for the first*
heaven and the first earth were passed away; and there was no
more sea. ***2.*** *And I John saw the holy city, new Jerusalem,*
coming down from God out of heaven, prepared as a bride
adorned for her husband. ***3.*** *And I heard a great voice out of*
heaven saying, Behold, the tabernacle of God [is] with men, and
he will dwell with them, and they shall be his people, and God
himself shall be with them, [and be] their God. ***4.*** *And God shall*
wipe away all tears from their eyes; and there shall be no more
death, neither sorrow, nor crying, neither shall there be any
more pain: for the former things are passed away. ***5.*** *And he*
that sat upon the throne said, Behold, I make all things new.
And he said unto me, Write: for these words are true and
faithful.

6. *And he said unto me, It is done. I am Alpha and Omega, the beginning and the end. I will give unto him that is athirst of the fountain of the water of life freely.* **7.** *He that overcometh shall inherit all things; and I will be his God, and he shall be my son..* **8.** *But the fearful, and unbelieving, and the abominable, and murderers, and whoremongers, and sorcerers, and idolaters, and all liars, shall have their part in the lake which burneth with fire and brimstone: which is the second death.* **9.** *And there came unto me one of the seven angels which had the seven vials full of the seven last plagues, and talked with me, saying, Come hither, I will shew thee the bride, the Lamb's wife.***10.** *And he carried me away in the spirit to a great and high mountain, and shewed me that great city, the holy Jerusalem, descending out of heaven from God,* **11.** *Having the glory of God: and her light was like unto a stone most precious, even like a jasper stone, clear as crystal;* **12.** *And had a wall great and high, and had twelve gates, and at the gates twelve angels, and names written thereon, which are the names of the twelve tribes of the children of Israel:* **13.** *On the east three gates; on the north three gates; on the south three gates; and on the west three gates.* **14.** *And the wall of the city had twelve foundations, and in them the names of the twelve apostles of the Lamb.* **15.** *And he that talked with me had a golden reed to measure the city, and the gates thereof, and the wall thereof.* **16.** *And the city lieth foursquare, and the length is as large as the breadth: and he measured the city with the reed, twelve thousand furlongs. The length and the breadth and the height of it are equal.* **17.** *And he measured the wall thereof, an hundred and forty and four cubits, [according to] the measure of a man, that is, of the angel.* **18.** *And the building of the wall of it was of jasper: and the city was pure gold, like unto clear glass.* **19.** *And the foundations of the wall of the city were garnished with all manner of precious stones. The first foundation was jasper; the second, sapphire; the third, a chalcedony; the fourth, an emerald;*

20. *The fifth, sardonyx; the sixth, sardius; the seventh, chrysolite; the eighth, beryl; the ninth, a topaz; the tenth, a chrysoprasus; the eleventh, a jacinth; the twelfth, an amethyst.* **21.** *And the twelve gates were twelve pearls; every several gate was of one pearl: and the street of the city was pure gold, as it were transparent glass.* **22.** *And I saw no temple therein: for the Lord God Almighty and the Lamb are the temple of it.* **23.** *And the city had no need of the sun, neither of the moon, to shine in it: for the glory of God did lighten it, and the Lamb is the light thereof.* **24.** *And the nations of them which are saved shall walk in the light of it: and the kings of the earth do bring their glory and honour into it.* **25.** *And the gates of it shall not be shut at all by day: for there shall be no night there.* **26.** *And they shall bring the glory and honour of the nations into it.* **27.** *And there shall in no wise enter into it any thing that defileth, neither whatsoever worketh abomination, or maketh a lie: but they which are written in the Lamb's book of life."* **(Revelation 21:1-27)**

1. *And he shewed me a pure river of water of life, clear as crystal, proceeding out of the throne of God and of the Lamb.* **2.** *In the midst of the street of it, and on either side of the river, was there the tree of life, which bare twelve manner of fruits, and yielded her fruit every month: and the leaves of the tree were for the healing of the nations.* **3.** *And there shall be no more curse: but the throne of God and of the Lamb shall be in it; and his servants shall serve him:* **4.** *And they shall see his face; and his name shall be in their foreheads.* **5.** *And there shall be no night there; and they need no candle, neither light of the sun; for the Lord God giveth them light: and they shall reign for ever and ever.* **6.** *And he said unto me, These sayings are faithful and true: and the Lord God of the holy prophets sent his angel to shew unto his servants the things which must shortly be done.*

7. *Behold, I come quickly: blessed is he that keepeth the sayings of the prophecy of this book.* **8.** *And I John saw these things, and heard them. And when I had heard and seen, I fell down to worship before the feet of the angel which shewed me these things.* **9.** *Then saith he unto me, See thou do it not: for I am thy fellowservant, and of thy brethren the prophets, and of them which keep the sayings of this book: worship God.* **10.** *And he saith unto me, Seal not the sayings of the prophecy of this book: for the time is at hand.* **11.** *He that is unjust, let him be unjust still: and he which is filthy, let him be filthy still: and he that is righteous, let him be righteous still: and he that is holy, let him be holy still.* **12.** *And, behold, I come quickly; and my reward is with me, to give every man according as his work shall be.* **13.** *I am Alpha and Omega, the beginning and the end, the first and the last.* **14.** *Blessed are they that do his commandments, that they may have right to the tree of life, and may enter in through the gates into the city.* **15.** *For without are dogs, and sorcerers, and whoremongers, and murderers, and idolaters, and whosoever loveth and maketh a lie.* **16.** *I Jesus have sent mine angel to testify unto you these things in the churches. I am the root and the offspring of David, and the bright and morning star.* **17.** *And the Spirit and the bride say, Come. And let him that heareth say, Come. And let him that is athirst come. And whosoever will, let him take the water of life freely.* **18.** *For I testify unto every man that heareth the words of the prophecy of this book, If any man shall add unto these things, God shall add unto him the plagues that are written in this book:* **19.** *And if any man shall take away from the words of the book of this prophecy, God shall take away his part out of the book of life, and out of the holy city, and [from] the things which are written in this book.*

20. *He which testifieth these things saith, Surely I come quickly. Amen. Even so, come, Lord Jesus.* ***21.*** *The grace of our Lord Jesus Christ be with you all. Amen.* **(Revelation 22:1-21.)**

"Powerful words that move mountains."

In the next few pages, I would like to compare heaven by looking at hell as an alternative for not believing in God Our Father.

DOES HELL EXIST?

Luke 16:23 "And in hell he lift up his eyes, being in torments. . ." The Bible continually tells us of a place called hell; there are over 162 references in the New Testament warning us and with over 70 reference warnings from our Lord Jesus Christ. **In Luke 16, Jesus Christ gives a frightening picture of hell.**

Luke 16:22-28 *". . . the rich man also died, and was buried; And **in hell** he lift up his eyes, **being in torments**, and seeth Abraham afar off, and Lazarus in his bosom. And he cried and said, Father Abraham, have mercy on me, and send Lazarus, that he may dip the tip of his finger in water, and cool my tongue; for I am tormented in this flame. But Abraham said, Son, remember that thou in thy lifetime receivedst thy good things, and likewise Lazarus evil things: but now he is comforted, and thou art tormented. And beside all this, between us and you there is a great gulf fixed: so that they which would pass from hence to you cannot; neither can they pass to us, that would come from thence. Then he said, I pray thee therefore, father, that thou wouldest send him to my father's house: For I have five brethren; that he may testify unto them, lest they also come into this place of torment."*

HELL IS A PLACE OF FIRE.
The man in Luke 16:24 cries: *". . .I am tormented in this flame."*

In Matthew 13:42, Jesus says: *"And shall cast them into a furnace of fire: there shall be wailing and gnashing of teeth."* In **Matthew 25:41, Jesus says**: *"Depart from me, ye cursed, into everlasting fire. . ."* Revelation 20:15 say, *" And whosoever was not found written in the book of life was cast into the lake of fire."*

WERE IS HELL?

When Jesus Christ died on the cross, He descended into hell. In Acts 2, Peter is speaking, verse 31, *". . . seeing this before spake of the resurrection of Christ, that his soul was not left in hell"*

When Jesus Christ died His soul went into hell.

In Matthew 12:40, **Jesus Christ says:** ***"For as Jonas was three days and three nights in the whale's belly: so shall the Son of man be three days and three nights in the heart of the earth."*** The Bible is clear Hell is inside the earth! Ephesians 4:9, says of Jesus: ***"Now that he ascended, what is it but that he also descended first into the lower parts of the earth."*** Thousands of years ago, the Bible described a place called hell in the heart of the earth that matches exactly what science is discovering.

THERE IS A HELL!

The Bible gives the account of people falling into hell alive! ***"And the earth opened her mouth, and swallowed them up, and their houses, and all the men that appertained unto Korah, and all their goods. They, and all that appertained to them, went down alive into the pit, and the earth closed upon them:"*** (Numbers 16:32-33.)

Inside this earth, this very moment, there are millions of lost, tormented souls burning, weeping, and wailing without any hope whatsoever! Although, the world tries to extinguish the cries and reality of hell, the truth of hell echoes throughout our world. Some people pretend to cover their ears and ignore that there is a hell, but it is there and we know it. *"they dig into hell."* ***Amos 9:2***

HELL IS TORMENT.

Jesus says of the man in Luke 16: 23 ***"And in hell he lift up his eyes, being in torments. . . "*** **24** ***". . . for I am tormented in this flame"*** **28** ***". . .Place of torment."*** It is humanly impossible to comprehend the Bible's description of hell, not even a horror movie could describe its frightening concept, with no crime scene with all its blood and gore could begin to match its horror. More then likely, people will see hell, they will smell hell, they will breath hell, and people will hear hell and they will feel hell. It will be beyond anything humanly imaginable! The Bible warns in Psalm 9:17, you will not only be in hell, you will be turned into hell! You will be literally hell! ***The wicked shall be turned into hell, and all the nations that forget God.*** Psalm 9:17

The Bible describes it as *weeping* **(Matt 8:12)**, *wailing* **(Matt 13:42)**, *gnashing of teeth* **(Matt 13:50),** *darkness* **(Matt 25:30)**, *flames* **(Luke 16:24)**, *burning* **(Isa 33:14)**, *torments* **(Luke 16:23)**, *everlasting punishment!* Jesus Christ says in Matthew 25:41, *"Depart from me, ye cursed, into everlasting fire, prepared for the devil and his angels."* In Matthew 13:42, Jesus says: *"And shall cast them into a furnace of fire: there shall be wailing and gnashing of teeth."*

Just read the following scriptures in your Bible that warns of the eternity and permanence of hell:

Everlasting fire — Matthew18:8, and 25:41
Everlasting punishment — Matthew 25:46
Everlasting chains — Jude 1:6
Eternal damnation — Mark 3:29

How Did Jesus Describe Hell? Jesus Christ spoke more on hell than any other subject, just look at how Jesus described hell: Fire (Matt 7:19, 13:40, 25:41) - Everlasting Fire (Matt 18:8, 25:41 - Eternal Damnation (Mark 3:29) - Hell Fire (Matt 5:22, 18:9, Mark 9:47) - Damnation (Matt 23:14, Mark 12:40, Luke 20:47) - Damnation of Hell (Matt 23:33) - Resurrection of Damnation (John 5:29) - Furnace of Fire (Matt 13:42,50) - The Fire That Never Shall Be Quench (Mark 9:43,45) - The Fire Is Not Quenched (Mark 9:44,46,48)- Wailing & Gnashing Of Teeth (Matt: 13:42,50) - Weeping & Gnashing Of Teeth (Matt 8:12, 22:13, 25:30) - Torments (Luke 16:23, 24) - Place Of Torment (Luke 16:28) - Outer Darkness (Matt 8:12, 22:13) - Everlasting Punishment (Matt 25:46)

What you must realize is God is a God of love and why would a GOD OF LOVE send us to hell? However, God is also a Holy God and because God is Holy, our sin will be condemned. Joshua 24:19 says, ***"... he is an Holy God;. . . he will NOT forgive your transgressions nor your sins."*** God does not want us in hell, for God is a God of love. Hell was not made for man as explained in; Matthew 25:41 says, hell was, *". . . prepared for the devil and his angels:"*

Because God is a God of Love, He sent His Son, Jesus Christ, to this earth to die a cruel death on the cross to pay the price a HOLY GOD demands for all of our sins. But this doesn't unnecessarily mean that you are truly saved by this alone, as you were already aware of this and it is up to you in leading a life through God's plan, or leading a life of sin. The choice is yours...

CHAPTER FIVE

God & His Prophecies

THE TRUTH BEHIND THE BIBLE

Getting back to my testimonial about the vision from Jesus, I decided to study the Bible more seriously; my intention was to gain a true understanding of His Spoken Word. I also felt the need to read other authors books and writings, including searching the Internet. The following information highlights many prophecies that were fulfilled in the old Testaments and I ask of you to read this important text, as it developed my faith and belief. Further on in this chapter you will see startling information that reveals the truth about Jesus our Lord and Savior and how scriptures hundreds of years before His time, reveal the end of His life as we know it. As I studied the world history, it added authenticity to the Bible. I found out that God gave to a Babylonian king an outline of history from his time until the end of the world. The Bible therefore had to be judged by the same standard as any other literature. The Bible is unique from all other works of literature. It was written over a period of 1600 years, in 66 books, by 40 authors. These authors were from all occupations. Two of them were half brothers of Jesus Christ, who did not believe His claims until after they witnessed His crucifixion and resurrection. The Bible was written in different locations, including the thrones of kings and the dungeons of jails. It was written on three different continents, Asia, Africa, and Europe, and in three different languages, Aramaic, Hebrew, and Greek. In spite of the diversity of its authors, as well as being written over a period of 1600 years, the fact is that most of these authors did not have access to the others' writings. Therefore, there was a consistency in the facts, as well as the theology of the Bible, and not one author criticized the other, with no dissenting opinions or footnotes.

Did you know that archaeologists, when in Israel, rely on the Bible to determine the locations of tells (sites) which has proved to be accurate. Historians have long acknowledged the Bible in accuracy. The Bible was transcribed many times over thousands of years; and critics claimed it was inaccurate, therefore not reliable. Before 1947, the oldest complete Bible was transcribed in 900A.D. Although the Jewish scribes were well disciplined in transcribing the Bible, it was nevertheless alleged that they must have transcribed it inaccurately. In 1947, a Bedouin shepherd lost a goat near the Dead Sea. He eventually found the goat on a ledge. To bring the goat into the flock, he threw rocks at it. Some of these rocks went into a cave, and the shepherd could hear the rocks breaking jars in this cave. He examined the cave and observed broken and unbroken jars. These jars contained the Dead Sea Scrolls. These Scrolls contained portions of all the books of the Hebrew Scriptures with the exception of the Book of Esther; they contained the entire book of Isaiah. A comparison was made of the Hebrew Scriptures, as transcribed in the Dead Sea Scrolls. This study revealed that the transcription in 900A.D. was 96% consistent with the Dead Sea Scrolls transcription, the remaining 4% being primarily mistakes in spelling. The Time Magazine dated August 14, 1989 stated: "The scrolls have also affected Bible translations read by millions of Jews and Christians. The caves contained portions of all books of the Old Testament except Esther, including a remarkably complete scroll of Isaiah that is 1,000 years older than any other surviving manuscript. Besides clearing up anomalies in several verses, the scrolls have demonstrated the remarkable accuracy which Jewish scribes preserved the text of the Bible."

BIBLICAL ARCHEOLOGY REVIEW, December 1992, an article by two Jewish scholars concerning the Dead Sea Scrolls stated: "Our Qumran text, 4Q521, is astonishingly, quite close to this Christian concept of the Messiah. Our text speaks not only of a single messianic figure but it also describes Him in extremely exalted terms, quite like the Christian view of Jesus as a cosmic agent. (That there was in fact an expectation of a single Messianic figure.) The Dead Sea transcribed 125 years before Christ. I then went in search of Jesus and my objective was to determine that Jesus is the Messiah based on Him fulfilling the messianic prophecies. Contained within the Hebrew Scriptures are over 300 prophecies concerning our Lord and Savior. These prophecies were written anywhere from 450 to over 2000 years before the birth of Jesus. They were so vivid that before the discovery of the Dead Sea Scrolls, antagonists argued, that ordinary men could not have written them. These antagonists felt if they were written before the birth of Jesus, it, with certainty, would have required a supernatural origin. Such skeptics flatly denied anything supernatural. The Dead Sea Scrolls established with certainty that all of these prophecies were written hundreds of years before the birth of Jesus. Their very argument proves the supernatural origin of these prophecies. I have selected a few of them for you to share in my findings.

Isaiah 7:14 "Therefore, the Lord Himself will give you a sign: The virgin will be with child and will give birth to a son." In those days, the people were wondering what signs God would give to them. Every female who became pregnant wondered if they were to bare the Son of God. During 285 BC, Plotemy Philadelphus commissioned 70 Jewish rabbis to transcribe the Hebrew Scriptures from Hebrew and Aramaic to Greek. These 70 scholars transcribed the Hebrew word "almah" to the Greek word "parthenos" both meaning virgin.

Current rabbis claim the word "almah" really means "young woman." ***Isaiah 7:14*** was intended to point out a "sign" so that Immanuel's" identity could be determined. If it meant "young woman" this sign could mean anybody in the world could bare the Son of God, and if so, would the mother realize whom she had given birth to? The Jewish rabbis wanted to be with the Son of God, but how can they locate the pregnant female? Millions of young Jewish women give birth to babies. The Jewish prophet Isaiah wrote in ***Isaiah 9:6-7:*** *"For a child will be born to us, a son will be given to us; and the government will rest upon His shoulders; and His name will be called Wonderful, Counselor, Mighty God, Eternal Father, Prince of Peace. There will be no end to the increase of His government or of peace. On the throne of David and over his Kingdom, to establish and uphold it with justice and righteousness from then on and forevermore. The zeal of the Lord of hosts will accomplish this."*

This passage describes prophetically that the Messiah would be true God and true man. The identity of the Messiah that he would be true God is revealed in verse 6 where it refers to Him as "Mighty God, Eternal Father." This same Messiah is described in verse 7 as being true man, because the Messiah will sit on the throne of David forevermore. This requires a worldly reign. Remember that Isaiah wrote this passage 750 years before the birth of Jesus Christ and before Isaiah and or anyone that had ever heard of Jesus Christ or Christianity. The Jewish prophet Micah wrote in ***Micah 5:2*** concerning the birth of the Messiah: ***"But as for you, Bethlehem Ephrathah, too little to be among the clans of Judah, from you One will go forth from Me to be ruler of Israel. His going forth are from long ago, from the days of eternity."***

Micah prophesied 450 years before the birth of Jesus that a man would be born in Bethlehem who had actually existed from "the days of eternity." I realized that this would have been a problem in fulfilling this prophecy through Mary and Joseph because they lived in Nazareth. Therefore, sometime before Jesus was born, they had to travel from Nazareth to Bethlehem. As I continually looked for loopholes, the reasoning was that Mary and Joseph went to Bethlehem after reading this prophecy, resulting in its fulfillment. After all, this was a well-known prophecy to all Jews. However, both, the Bible as well as other history books (the Bible, among other things, is a history book) recorded that Mary and Joseph traveling to Bethlehem was not voluntary. Caesar Augustus, a pagan and ruler of Rome, required that all Jews of the House of David travel to Bethlehem for the purpose in taking a census so they could be taxed. One of the great historians Dr. Luke, set forth in ***Luke 2:1-5: "Now it came about in those days that a decree went out from Caesar Augustus, that a census be taken of all the inhabited earth."***

This was the first census taken while Quirinius was governor of Syria and all were the people needed to register for the census, everyone, to there own city. Joseph also went up from Galilee, from the city of Nazareth, to Judea, the city of David, which is called Bethlehem. Because he was of the house and family of David, in order to register he needed to go with Mary who was with child. In 1923 at Ankara Turkey, a Roman inscription was discovered that recorded there were three great censuses initiated during the reign of Caesar Augustus. The middle census occurring in 7B.C. History records that there were petitions sent to Rome by the Jews protesting that they had to travel this long distance to be counted for this census. Due to this protest there was a delay of approximately three years before the census was carried out, resulting in the census being taken in 4B.C.

That year is the precise year that Jesus Christ was born in Bethlehem. There were twelve, different cities to which the Jews were required to go for the purpose in taking this census. "Each of the 12 tribes going to a different city." This is verified in the passage from Luke; which states; ***"and all were proceeding to register for the census everyone to his own city."*** Therefore, God, through the prophet, Micah, had 1 chance out of 12 to guess the correct city where Jesus Christ, being of the tribe of Judah (house of David) would be born. The last two sentences of the Micah passage describe who was to be born in Bethlehem: ***"His goings forth are from long ago, from the days of eternity."*** No one but God has existed from the days of eternity. This is a prophecy that God, Himself, would be born in Bethlehem and another prophecy that the Messiah would be true God and true man when God the Son became incarnate. At the time that Micah wrote this prophecy, Bethlehem Ephrathah was the classical name for the city of Bethlehem. The Jewish prophet Zechariah prophesied ***Zechariah 9:9*** *"rejoice greatly, O daughter of Zion! Shout in triumph, O daughter of Jerusalem! Behold, your king is coming to you; He is just and endowed with salvation, humble, and mounted on a donkey, even on a colt, the foal of a donkey."*

The fulfillment of the above prophecy occurred when Jesus, the Messiah, entered Jerusalem mounted on a "donkey," also utilizing a "colt," on Palm Sunday. (***Matthew 21:1-3.***) One of the most profound Messianic prophecies was written by Isaiah 750 years before the birth of Jesus in ***Isaiah 52:13-53:12.*** This prophecy speaks of the Servant of Jehovah who undergoes great suffering, who dies a death as a result of being pierced, who vicariously suffers this death for His people, which death is for the sin of others, and finally, this suffering servant is resurrected from the dead. This prophecy describes in detail the suffering, death, and resurrection of Jesus the Messiah.

Isaiah 52:13-15 *"Behold, My servant will prosper, He will be high and lifted up, and greatly exalted. Just as many were astonished at you, My people, so His appearance was marred more than any man and His form more than the sons of men. Thus He will sprinkle many nations, kings will shut their mouths on account of Him; for what had not been told them they will see, and what they had not heard they will understand."*

This speaks of the suffering servant being "lifted up" implying He would be resurrected. In verse 14 the suffering servant who is resurrected is further identified as being "marred more than any man" and Jesus Christ, was marred more than any other man when He was scourged, (whipped), crowned with thorns and nails pierced His body. (***John 19:3***) During Jesus' life, very few did believe His message, thus fulfilling this prophecy. The phrase "the arm of the Lord" implies the Son of God and asks the question to whom has the Son of God been revealed? ***Isaiah 53:2*** *"For He grew up before Him like a tender shoot, and like a root out of parched ground."* This verse speaks of Jesus' childhood and discusses this "root" growing up out of "parched ground" which implies the virgin birth. It is miraculous for a root to grow out of parched ground, just as it is miraculous for the Messiah to be born of "her seed" as set forth in ***Genesis 3:15***. Yeshua, Jesus was the only person born of a woman's seed. Humankind is always born of a man's seed. The pronoun "He" refers to the Messiah and the pronoun "Him" refers to God the Father.

Isaiah 53:2 *"He has no stately form or majesty that we should look upon Him, nor appearance that we should be attracted to Him."*

Jesus Christ would not have any "stately form or majesty" being born in a stable, working in His youth as a carpenter, being raised in Nazareth, which was so unimportant it was never mentioned in the Hebrew Scriptures, and being only an itinerant preacher. Having no "stately form" implies He was a young, Jewish man indistinguishable from thousands of other young Jewish men. ***Zechariah 9:9*** prophetically confirms this prophecy, and prophesies concerning the humility of Jesus Christ: "*Behold your king is coming to you; He is just and endowed with salvation. Humble, mounted on a donkey, even on a colt, the foal of a donkey."* Kings do not ride donkeys. They ride in chariots. Jesus, as a humble servant, fulfilled this prophecy on Palm Sunday when He entered Jerusalem on a donkey. (***John 12:12-14***) In the first advent of Jesus Christ, *"He was to come as a suffering servant and not as a conquering King."* In the Second Advent of Christ at the end of the tribulation, just before the Messianic Kingdom, *"He will again return this time as a conquering King."* "It was the failure to understand this distinction that led to considerable confusion concerning Jesus Christ particularly by the Jews."

Isaiah 53:3 *"He was despised and forsaken of men, a man of sorrows, and acquainted with grief; and like one from whom men hide their face, He was despised, and we did not esteem Him."*

This prophecy describes the social life of Jesus the Messiah. The prophecy that He would be "forsaken of men" was vividly fulfilled in ***Matthew 26:56*** where Jesus' disciple, Matthew, admitted that when Jesus was arrested in the Garden of Gethsemane, he and the other disciples "left Him and fled."

Throughout the Bible, the authors confess their shortcomings and sins. ***Isaiah 53:4,5,6,10,11 and l2.*** (This reflects the message of the Cross- that the Messiah was to be the Lamb of God. That would take away the sins of the world by causing all the sins of the world to fall upon Him: *"Surely our grief's He Himself bore, And our sorrows He carried; Yet we ourselves esteemed Him stricken, Smitten of God, and afflicted. But He was pierced through for our transgressions, He was crushed for our iniquities; the chastening for our well being fell upon Him, and by His scourging, we are healed.*

All of us like sheep have gone astray, each of us has turned to his own way; but the Lord has caused the iniquity of us all to fall on Him; If He would render Himself as a guilt offering, My servant, will justify the many, Yet He, Himself, bore the sin of many." The message of the cross: ***Zechariah 12:10***. *"And I will pour out on the house of David and on the inhabitants of Jerusalem, the Spirit of grace and of supplication, so that they will look on Me whom they have pierced; and they will mourn for Him, as one mourns for an only son, and they will weep bitterly over Him, like the bitter weeping over a firstborn.* The previous two prophecies were fulfilled when Jesus' body was "pierced" and "crushed" by being nailed to the cross and was scourged (whipped) by the Roman soldiers. This whipping by the Roman soldiers consisted of lashing Jesus' body with a whip made of 40 strands of leather at the end of which was pieces of glass. Many died from this "scourging" alone. Isaiah prophesied that the suffering servant would humbly submit to unjust treatment and would not speak a word in His defense. ***Isaiah 53:7****"He was oppressed and He was afflicted, yet He did not open His mouth; like a lamb that is led to slaughter, and like a sheep that is silent before its shearers, so He did not open His mouth."*

The fulfillment of the above prophecy: ***Matthew 27:13-14*** *Then Pilate said to Him, "Do you not hear how many things they testify against you?" And He did not answer him with regard to even a single charge, so that the governor was quite amazed."*

By oppression and judgment, He was taken away. It was prophesied that when the Messiah was judged, and thereafter crucified, it would be by oppression. Studies have established that the trial of Jesus was by oppression. Perhaps the most compelling and convicting prophecy in Isaiah was the following, written 750 years before the birth of Jesus: ***Isaiah 53:9*** *"His grave was assigned with wicked men. Yet He was with a rich man in His death."* Jesus Christ grave was assigned to be with wicked men, because He was destined to be buried with two thieves in a common burial plot set-aside exclusively for wicked men outside of Jerusalem. Was Jesus buried in this grave with wicked men and was He with a rich man in His death? The answer is found in Matthew where it is revealed that Joseph of Arimathea, a rich man, asked Pontius Pilate for the body of Jesus and thus prevented Him from being buried in a grave with wicked men. This rich man then took the body of Jesus and buried Him in his tomb:

Matthew 27:57-60 *"And when it was evening, there came a rich man from Arimathea, named Joseph, who himself had also become a disciple of Jesus. This man came to Pilate and asked for the body of Jesus. Then Pilate ordered it to be given over to him. And Joseph took the body and wrapped it in a clean linen cloth, and laid it in his own new tomb, which he had hewn out in the rock; and he rolled a large stone against the entrance of the tomb and went away."*

Isaiah prophesied that God the Father so loved the world (see ***John 3:16***) that He was pleased to render the suffering servant as a guilt offering for the sins of the people:

"But the Lord was pleased to crush Him, putting Him to grief; if He would render himself as a guilt offering; He will see His offspring, He will prolong His days." ***Isaiah 53:12*** *"Because He poured out Himself to death, and was numbered with the transgressors; yet, He, Himself, bore the sin of many, and interceded for the transgressors."* The prophecies foretell that the suffering servant who would render Himself as a "guilt offering," would be crushed to death and would thereafter be resurrected from the dead: "He will see His offspring, He will prolong his days." The only way He would see His offspring after being killed as a guilt offering was by being resurrected from the dead.

"The Servant will be blessed above all because He so loved the world that He willingly and voluntarily suffered and died for the sins of the people; was humble enough to let others consider Him to be a sinner when in fact He was without sin; and He bore the sins of many." ***Isaiah 53:12*** *"Therefore, I will allot Him a portion with the great, and He will divide the booty with the strong; because He poured out Himself to death, and was numbered with the transgressors; yet He Himself bore the sin of many and interceded for the transgressors."*

The Dead Sea Scrolls, supra, established that the Book of Isaiah contained in the Jewish Bible was written hundreds of years before the birth of Jesus. Until approximately 1100 AD, there was agreement among Jewish scholars and Rabbis that the Isaiah prophecy referred to the Messiah. Antagonists of Christ must explain away this prophecy as not being Messianic. To accomplish this, after 1100A.D the majority of Jewish scholars and Rabbis took the position that this prophecy did not speak of a specific person but, rather, the Jewish people. However, many Jewish scholars and Rabbis admitted that Isaiah was speaking of the Messiah. Fruchtenbaum in "**JESUS WAS A JEW**" developed the following argument: important proof as to whom this passage referred is the consistent use of pronouns. A distinction is made between the plural "we," "us" and "our" and the singular "He," "Him" and "His." Consistently the use of "we," "us" and "our" in the passage must refer collectively to Isaiah the prophet together with the Jewish people to whom Isaiah was speaking. ***"His grave was assigned with wicked men, yet He was with a rich man in His death, because He had done no violence, nor wasthere any deceit in His mouth."*** In Isaiah 53:4-9, the use of the pronouns "we," "us" and "our" refer to the Jewish people, including Isaiah. Isaiah is thus speaking to the Jewish people as a whole. He includes himself with the Jewish people. Isaiah represents the Messiah or the suffering servant in a different category by using the singular and personal pronouns "He', "Him" and "His". He is the one who is suffering for us. He is the one God on whom we lay our sins. He is the one who is going to die for our sins so that we can have salvation through Him. The constant use of these pronouns excludes the suffering servant from being Israel. Rather, the suffering servant is the Messiah, Himself. The second area of proof is in the closing sentence of verse 8 which also serves to exclude Israel from being the suffering servant: ***"He was cut off out of the land of the living for the transgression of my people to whom the stroke was due."***

As Isaiah views the death of the suffering servant, it was for the sins of "my people". No one questions Isaiah's people as being the Jews. Moreover, if "my people" are the Jews, they cannot be at the same time the singular suffering "servant" because in the same sentence, distinction is made between "He" and "my people". Hence, the suffering servant must refer to the individual Messiah. The third proof is that throughout the entire passage the suffering servant is portrayed as a singular human personality. The fourth proof is that the suffering servant is presented in the verses as an innocent sufferer. It is easy to see how this can be true of the Messiah but it is impossible for the innocent sufferer to apply to the Jewish people or, for that matter, any people, because none are innocent. The prophet Isaiah never told the Jews that they would suffer for being innocent but rather that they would suffer for their sins. God punished Israel many times and in various ways and it was always for their sins and not because they were all innocent. The fifth proof is the suffering servant being portrayed as a voluntary, willing, and silent sufferer. He willingly submits to the suffering He undergoes and voices no complaint as to the injustice being suffered. The Jewish people throughout Biblical history could not be accused of being silent. ***(See Numbers 11:1, 14:2-3, 14:27 and 16:13-14.)*** The sixth proof is the passage describing the Messiah suffering death. He suffers for the sake of others, both Jews and Gentiles that they need not suffer for their sins.

Nowhere in the scriptures or in Jewish history, do we ever see Israel suffering for Gentiles? The seventh proof is crucial, according to Isaiah, the suffering servant dies, and, of course, the Jewish people are alive. In fact, God, in other passages of the Bible, supra, pages 12 and 13 promises that the survival and identity of the Jewish people is to be everlasting.

Psalm 22 "A band of evil doers has encompassed me; they pierced my hands and my feet. I can count all my bones. They look, they stare at me; they divide my garments among them, and for my clothing they cast lots."

This passage can be recited to virtually any person on earth and they will conclude it speaks of the crucifixion of Jesus. Amazingly, it is from ***Psalm 22:16,*** which was written by King David, a thousand years before the birth of Jesus! At the time King David made this prophecy, the Jews had never heard of death by crucifixion. The means of enforcing capital punishment by the Jews was stoning. "In order for this prophecy to be fulfilled, some country which utilized death by crucifixion would have to conquer Israel." This was fulfilled when Rome conquered Israel and, then, the prophecy was historically in a position to be fulfilled. King David, in the same Psalm, which discusses the same person who was pierced, prophecies in verses 14 and 15: ***"I am poured out like water, and all my bones are out of joint; my heart is like wax; it is melted within me. My strength is dried up like a potsherd, and my tongue cleaves to my jaws; and Thou dost lay me in the dust of death."***

This prophecy sets forth what will happen to the Messiah, when being pierced and crucified: "He will be **poured** out like **water**." **2.** "All his **bones** will be out of **joint**." **3. "**His **heart** turns to a substance like **wax** and it is melted within him." **4.** "His **strength** while dying becomes **dried** up like a potsherd." **5.** "His **tongue cleaves** to his **jaws** during his **death."**

I asked myself, do any of these statements bare any fact to a person that suffers death by crucifixion.

"I AM POURED OUT LIKE WATER" AND "MY HEART IS LIKE WAX; IT IS MELTED WITHIN ME"

In order to determine the cause of death when a person is crucified, Dr. Samuel Houghton of the University of Dublin conducted a series of experiments to determine precisely that. Dr. Houghton, as a result, of these experiments concluded that when a person is crucified, he often dies from a ruptured heart. When he dies from a ruptured heart, the pericardial sac that surrounds the heart bursts and if the crucified person is pierced in, the side one can observe blood followed by water coming from this wound. Dr. Houghton established that this prophecy, which states that the person being crucified, would be "poured out like water," his heart would be "like wax" and it would be "melted within" him is physiologically sound. An eyewitness at the foot of the cross of Jesus, John the apostle confirmed this prophecy when he actually observed the side of Jesus being pierced and out came blood followed by water.

John 19:33-35 *"But coming to Jesus, when they saw that He was already dead, they did not break His legs; but one of the soldiers pierced His side with a spear, and immediately there came out blood and water. And he who has seen has borne witness, and his witness is true; and he knows that he is telling the truth, so that you also may believe."*

John was not a graduate pathologist from the University of Jerusalem but, rather, a fisherman and was more then likely very perplexed as to his observations. The only thing that he knew was that when he was standing at the foot of the cross of Jesus, a spear went into His side, and he observed blood and then water flow from this wound. Dr. Houghton confirmed why this observation is so piercingly convicting as to the truth of Jesus' crucifixion and John's eyewitness testimony.

Let us review the agonizing experience that Jesus had to go through from king David in which he wrote about the prophecy in ***Psalm 22.*** **"ALL MY BONES ARE OUT OF JOINT"** The next physiological condition to be experienced by the Messiah, when crucified, was that all of His bones would be "out of joint." This has been confirmed by observations that when a person is hanging from a cross, the force of gravity pulls his joints apart so that they are in fact "out of joint. **"STRENGTH IS DRIED UP LIKE A POTSHERD"** The Messiah, when being pierced and crucified, would experience His "strength" being 'dried up like a potsherd" or dried cow dung, thus, fulfilling this prophecy. **"MY TONGUE CLEAVES TO MY JAWS"** And finally, it was prophesied that the tongue of the Messiah, when being crucified, "cleaves' to His "jaws." A person being crucified experiences such extreme thirsts that his tongue "cleaves" to his "jaws."

PROPHECIES CONCERNING JESUS

Psalm 22:17: "I can count all my bones." When the Messiah was crucified and looked to the ground, His bones being out of joint could be observed and counted.

Psalm 22:18: "They divide my garments among them, and for my clothing they cast lots." This prophecy was fulfilled not by Jesus' disciples or others who believed in Him but by pagan Roman soldiers.

This fulfillment is recorded in ***Matthew 27:35 "And when they had crucified Him, they divided up His garments among themselves, casting lots."***

Psalm 34:20, prophetically, states what John observed, that Jesus' legs would not be broken: ***"He keeps all His bones, not one of them is broken".***

Psalm 22:1 states: ***"My God, my God, why hast thou forsaken me?"*** Jesus uttered these words from the cross in ***Matthew 27:46:*** Jesus recited these exact words of ***Psalm 22*** saying that Psalm 22 speaks of Him.

Psalm 22:7-8 prophecies that the Messiah, from the cross, will observe that all who see me, sneer at me and they wag the head. ***"All who see me, sneer at me; they separate with the lip, they wag the head, saying, "Commit yourself to the Lord; let Him deliver him; let Him rescue him, because He delights in Him."***

The fulfillment of this prophecy is recorded in ***Mark 15:29 "And those passing by were hurling abuse at Him, wagging their heads, and saying, "Ha! You who are going to destroy the temple and rebuild it in three days."*** And again in ***Luke 23:35 "And the people stood by, looking on, and even the rulers were sneering at Him, saying, "He saved others; let Him save Himself if this is the Christ of God, His Chosen One."***

There are over 300 prophecies concerning the Messiah that were fulfilled, and could only be fulfilled by the life of Jesus Christ. Someone calculated the mathematical probability of a person fulfilling just eight of the 300 prophecies, by chance. The conclusion was that there was one chance in 1017. So that we can understand the enormity of this number, if silver dollars two feet high covered the entire state of Texas, and only one was made in 1989, the mathematical probability of a person selecting that single 1989 silver dollar would be impossible. "In other words, impossible." What is the reason for God outlining in such detail the prophecies concerning His Son and their fulfillment?

That question is answered in ***John 20:31 "But these have been written that you may believe that Jesus is the Christ, the Son of God; and that believing, you may have life in His name."***

JESUS VERIFIED THAT ALL THINGS WRITTEN ABOUT HIM IN THE LAW OF MOSES, THE PROPHETS AND THE PSALM WERE FULFILLED.

Jesus stated in the Bible: ***"Now He said to them, These are My words which I spoke to you while I was still with you, that all things which are written about Me in the Law of Moses and the Prophets and the Psalm must be fulfilled."***

"***Then He opened their minds to understand the Scriptures."*** **(Luke 24:44-45.)**

Jesus the Messiah:

The Biblical credentials and lineage of Jesus the Messiah setting forth His forefathers 750 to 1,000 years before His birth are found in the following passages of the Hebrew Scriptures: The Messiah will be a Jew and come through only the seed of Abraham. ***(Genesis 22:18.)***

Abraham had eight sons, including Isaac and Ishmael, and the Messiah was prophesied to come only through Isaac. ***(Genesis 26:4.)*** Isaac had two sons, Jacob and Esau, and it was prophesied that the Messiah must come through only Jacob. ***(Genesis 28:14.)*** Jacob had 12 sons, from whom came the 12 tribes of Israel, and it was prophesied that the Messiah must come through only the tribe of Judah. ***(Genesis 49:10.)***

Of the thousands of families in the tribe of Judah, it was prophesied that the Messiah must come through only the family of Jesse. ***(Isaiah 11:1-2.)***

Jesse had eight sons, and it was prophesied that the Messiah must come through only Jesse's youngest son, David. ***Psalm 132:11.***

In ***Matthew 1:1-17*** the genealogy of Jesus Christ, through Joseph Is set forth through the following forty ancestors: Abraham, Isaac, Jacob, Judah, Perez, Heron, Ram, Amanda, Nacho, Salmon, Boaz, Orbed, Jesse, David, Solomon, Jeroboam, Abuja, Assay, Jehoshaphat, Joram, Uzziah, Jotham, Ahaz, Hezekiah, Manasseh, Amon, Josiah, Jeconiah, Shealtiel, Zerubbabel, Abiud, Eliakim, Azor, Zadok, Achim, Eliud, Eleazar, Matthan, Jacob and Joseph. The genealogy of Jesus Christ, through Mary, is set forth through the following 73 ancestors in Luke 3:23-38: Matthat, Melchi, Jannai, Joseph, Mattathias, Amos, Nahum, Hesli, Naggai, Maath, Mattathias, Semein, Josech, Joda, Joanan, Rhesa, Zerubbabel, Shealtiel, Neri, Melchi, Addi, Cosam, Elmadam, Er, Joshua, Eliezer, Jorim, Matthat, Levi, Simeon, Joseph, Jonam, Eliakim, Melea, Menna, Mattatha, Nathan, David, Jesse, Boaz, Salmon, Nahshon, Amminadab, Admin, Ram, Hezron, Perez, Juda, Jacob, Isaac, Abraham, Terah, Nahor, Serug, Reu, Peleg, Heber, Shelah, Cainan, Arphaxad, Shem, Noah, Lamech, Methuselah, Enoch, Jared, Mahalaleel, Cainan, Enos, Neosh, Seth, and Adam who was the son of God. What is the point in setting forth all of these ancestors? Answer: So that we can know the truth that Jesus, the Son of God is irrefutably the Messiah.

Until the destruction of the Jewish temple in 70A.D, the genealogy of not only Jesus but of each of His ancestors was available in the temple for anyone to study. Jesus claimed his genealogy through each of them. Contained in the Jewish second temple, which was destroyed in 70A.D, by the Romans were the genealogical records of all of the Jews dating back to the time of Abraham.

1 Chronicles 9:1 establishes the keeping of these genealogical records: *"So all Israel was enrolled by genealogies; and behold, they are written in the Book of the Kings of Israel. And Judah was carried away into exile to Babylon for their unfaithfulness."*

Jesus Christ claimed that He alone fulfilled the prophecies set forth in the Hebrew Scriptures.

Matthew 5:17-18 *"Do not think that I came to abolish the Law or the Prophets; I did not come to abolish, but to fulfill. For truly I say to you, until heaven and earth pass away, not the smallest letter or stroke shall pass away from the Law, until all is accomplished."*

The Bible is the result of a mysterious combination of the divine and the human, as was Jesus Christ. As the human mind is incapable of fully explaining the incarnation, so it cannot fully explain the Bible. In writing the various books of the Bible, the authors' own personalities had full play, and their own style and vocabulary are reflected in the finished product. Yet the Bible is nevertheless, "inspired by God."

2 Timothy 3:16,17 *"While men did the speaking, they did so as they were moved by the Holy Spirit."*

2 Peter 1:21 *"The Bible is, therefore in a special sense the Word of God."*

Evidence of the Bibles inspirations included prophecy, archeology, cohesive unity, accuracy, and Christ revealed. In the Bible, it gives illustrations for what are the essentials of Christianity: Recognize that God loves you with an immense love and desires to save you. **(2 Peter 3:9:1.)**

Acknowledge that you are a sinner, lost without Jesus Christ. **(Jeremiah 17:9, Roman 3:23 and 6:23.)**

Accept that salvation is a gift offered freely through Jesus. It is not something to be earned by righteous deeds or good works. **(Ephesians 2:8, Romans 3:24-27.)**

Repent of any known sins, confessing them to Jesus. **Act 3:19, and 1 John 1:19**.

Believe that God for Christ's sake has forgiven you. As you surrender your life to Jesus, you are forgiven and accepted. The gift of eternal life is yours by faith. **(Ephesians 1:4-7, and John 5:11-13.)**

Since you are now a child of Christ, His precious possession, He will begin to work miraculous changes in your life through His Holy Spirit. **(John 1:12, and Corinthians 5:17.)**

Our loving Savior has pledged to guide us from earth to heaven. You may fall, but remember Jesus is there to pick you up, and get you started on the road to heaven again.

JESUS' PROMISES TO ALL OF HIS FOLLOWERS

In the bible Jesus our Lord and Savior made a number of promises to his followers that still stands today for that that believe and have faith. Jesus promised that when we love Him, God would also love us: ***"They who have my commandments and keep them are those who love me; and those who love me will be loved by my Father, and I will love them and reveal myself to them."*** **(John 14:21)**

"As the Father has loved me, so I have loved you; abide in my love. If you keep my commandments, you will abide in my love, just as I have kept my Father's commandments and abide in his love." **(John 15:9-10)**

"For God so loved the world that he gave his only Son, so that everyone who believes in him may not perish but may have eternal life." **(John 3:16)**

"I in them and you in me, that they may become completely one, so that the world may know that you have sent me and have loved them even as you have loved me." **(John 17:23)**

Jesus through His love and Compassion wants to give us a fresh start in life, were we can be forgiven for our worldly sins providing that we have true belief in Him:

"Which one of you, having a hundred sheep and losing one of them, does not leave the ninety-nine in the wilderness and go after the one that is lost until he finds it? When he has found it, he lays it on his shoulders and rejoices. And when he comes home, he calls together his friends and neighbors, saying to them, 'Rejoice with me, for I have found my sheep that was lost.' Just so, I tell you, there will be more joy in heaven over one sinner who repents than over ninety-nine righteous persons who need no repentance." **(Luke 15: 4-7)**

"Everyone who commits sin is a slave to sin. The slave does not have a permanent place in the household; the Son has a place there forever. So if the Son makes you free, you will be free indeed." **(John 8:34 -36)**

"Whenever you stand praying, forgive, if you have anything against anyone; so that your Father in heaven may also forgive you your trespasses." **(Mark 11:25)**

"For if you forgive others their trespasses, your heavenly Father will also forgive you; but if you do not forgive others, neither will your Father forgive your trespasses." **(Matthew 6:14-15)**

"Do not judge, and you will not be judged; do not condemn, and you will not be condemned. Forgive, and you will be forgiven; give, and it will be given to you. A good measure, pressed down, shaken together, running over, will be put in to your lap; for the measure you give will be the measure you get back." **Luke 6:37-38)**

"I have come as light into the world, so that everyone who believes in me should not remain in the darkness." **(John 12:46)**

In fellowship with Jesus, he wants us to have faith in God and his Word to fulfill the promises that he made whilst on this earth: ***"Have faith in God. Truly I tell you, if you say to this mountain, 'be taken up and thrown into the sea,' and if you do not doubt in your heart, but believe that what you say will come to pass, it will be done for you. So I tell you, whatever you ask for in prayer, believe that you have received it, and it will be yours."*** **(Mark 11:22-24)**

"For truly I tell you, if you have faith the size of a mustard seed, you will say to this mountain, 'Move from here to there,' and it will move; and nothing will be impossible for you." **(Matthew 17: 20)**

"If you abide in me, and my words abide in you, ask for whatever you wish, and it will be done for you." **(John 15:7)**

"Is there anyone among you who, if your child asks for bread, will give a stone? Or if the child asks for a fish, will give a snake? If you then, who are evil, know how to give good gifts to your children, how much more will your Father in heaven given good things to those who ask him." **(Matthew 7:9-11)**

Jesus promised us eternal life for following Him in his footsteps to lead a life of Christian values to others, also to have belief in Him and the spoken word: ***"For God so loved the world that he gave his one and only Son, that whoever believes in him shall not perish but have eternal life."*** **(John 3:16)**

"My sheep hear my voice. I know them, and they follow me. I give them eternal life, and they will never perish. No one will snatch them out of my hand." **John 10: 27)**

"Very truly, I tell you, whoever believes has eternal life." **(John 6:47)**

"I am the resurrection and the life. Those who believe in me, even though they die, will live, and everyone who lives and believes in me will never die." **(John 11: 25-26)**

"And this is eternal life, that they may know you, the only true God, and Jesus Christ whom you have sent." **(John 17:3)**

"Very truly, I tell you, anyone who hears my word and believes him who sent me has eternal life, and does not come under judgment, but has passed from death to life." **(John 5:24)**

"This is indeed the will of my Father, that all who see the Son and believe in him may have eternal life; and I will raise them up on the last day." **(John 6:39-40)**

Jesus promises us that, God's Spirit will reside in us:
"And I will ask the Father, and he will give you another Advocate, to be with you forever. This is the Spirit of truth, whom the world cannot receive, because it neither sees him nor knows him. You know him, because he abides with you, and he will be in (alt: among) you." **(John 14: 16-17)**

"But the Advocate, the Holy Spirit, whom the Father will send in my name, will teach you everything, and remind you of all that I have said to you." **(John 14:26)**

"When they bring you to trial and hand you over, do not worry before hand about what you are to say; but say whatever is given you at that time, for it is not you who speak, but the Holy Spirit." **(Mark 13:11)**

"And remember, I am with you always, to the end of the age." **(Matthew 28:20)**

"If you then, who are evil, know how to give good gifts to your children, how much more will the heavenly Father give the Holy Spirit to those who ask him!" **(Matthew 7: 9-11)**

Jesus promised that He would leave peace with us for believing in Him: ***"Peace I leave with you; my peace I give to you."*** **(John 14:27)**

"...in me you may have peace. In the world you face persecution. But take courage; I have conquered the world!" **(John 16:33)**

"Come to me, all you that are weary and are carrying heavy burdens, and I will give you rest. Take my yoke upon you, and learn from me; for I am gentle and humble in heart, and you will find rest for your souls. For my yoke is easy, and my burden is light." **(Matthew 11: 28-30)**

Jesus promises us rewards in heaven for our fellowship and belief in Him: ***"You lack one thing; go, sell what you own, and give the money to the poor, and you will have treasure in heaven; then come, follow me."*** **(Mark 10:21)**

"Truly I tell you, there is no one who has left house or brothers or sisters of mother or father or children or fields, for my sake and for the sake of the good news, who will not receive a hundredfold now in this age - houses, brothers and sisters, mothers and children, and fields with persecutions - and in the age to come eternal life. But many who are first will be last, and the last will be first." **(Mark 10:29-31)**

"Blessed are you when people hate you, and when they exclude you, revile you, and defame you on account of the Son of Man. Rejoice in that day and leap for joy, for surely your reward is great in heaven; for that is what their ancestors did to the prophets." **(Luke 6:22)**

"But love your enemies, do good, and lend, expecting nothing in return. Your reward will be great, and you will be children of the Most High; for he is kind to the ungrateful and the wicked." **(Luke 6:35)**

For all of the promises that Jesus made to us, all He is asking in return is:

1. LOVE & OBEY GOD.
2. LOVE & OBEY HIM.
3. LOVE ONE ANOTHER.
4. FORGIVE ONE ANOTHER.
5. INVITE JESUS TO BE CLOSE TO YOU.
6. BELIEVE JESUS FOR WHO HE CLAIMED TO BE.
7. HAVE FAITH, TRUST IN GOD.

BACKGROUND TO JESUS

Jesus was born in Bethlehem and raised in Nazareth, 2000 years ago and for the first 30 years of his life, Jesus lived a traditional Jewish life, working as a carpenter. During this time, the Romans ran the country under the dictatorship of Caesar. In his thirties, Jesus' reputation spread nationwide. The Romans and other rulers of Israel, including religious group leaders were very much aware of Jesus and his style of preaching. Jesus Key messages were: God loves you and he resides with you, love one another, value each and every person, the Kingdom of God has come to earth, the judgment to heaven and hell, and finally God forgives them that ask for forgiveness.

Jesus' most controversial act was that he repeatedly claimed to be God, which was a forbidden Jewish law to make such a claim. The religious leaders then request that the Roman government would execute Jesus. According to well over 500 witnesses, Jesus rose from the dead three days after his brutal murder, and over the next 40 days, journeyed in both the southern and northern towns and cities of Israel. After this Jesus then went back to Jerusalem were hc was executed and witnesses saw him leave this earth to be in Heaven. To many people this was proof enough that Jesus claim to be God was real. Since then, Jesus' followers have been increasing. 100 years later, people throughout the roman empire (Asia Minor, Europe) became followers of Jesus. In 325 AD, the following of Jesus through Christianity became the official religion of the Roman Emperor Constantine. Within 500 years, even Greece's temples of their own Greek gods were transformed into churches, for followers of Jesus.

THE RECORDS OF JESUS' SUPERNATURAL ACTS

(All recorded in Matthew, Mark, Luke, and John in the Bible.)

1. Jesus turns water into wine. 2. The temple taxes (money) were placed in the mouth of a fish. 3. Jesus fills Peter's net with fish, when there was none. 4. Jesus invisibly escapes through an angry crowd. 5. Jesus turns food scraps into meal for 5,000 people. 6. Jesus causes a fig tree to wither. 7. Jesus calms a raging storm. 8. Jesus walks on water. 9. Non-Jewish woman's daughter cleansed of demon-possession. 10. Man cleansed of demon-possession. 11. Boy cleansed of demon-possession. 12. Two demon-possessed men cleansed simultaneously. 13. Mute: man's speech restored. 14. Deaf and Mute: man's hearing and speech restored. 15. Crippled: woman's spine straightened after 18 years. 16. Crippled: lame man (at Bethesda pool) walks after 38 years. 17. Crippled: paralytic man (carried by friends) healed. 18. Crippled: a man's withered hand restored. 19. Blind, Mute and Demon-possessed: man healed. 20. Blind: man born blind receives sight. 21. Blind: two men's sight restored simultaneously. 22. Blind: another two men's sight restored simultaneously. 23. Ten people healed of Leprosy. 24. A man healed of Leprosy. 25. Woman's chronic blood hemorrhaging stops. 26. Healed Malchus' severed ear. 27. Healed Peter's mother-in-law healed. 28. The centurion's servant healed of paralysis and suffering. 29. Royal official's son remotely healed. 30. Widow's son rose from the dead. 31. Lazarus rose from the dead. 32. Jairus' daughter rose from the dead.

THE MAIN WITNESSES OF JESUS

John - was a Jewish fisherman from the northern Israeli town of Capernaum, where Jesus spent most of his final three years. John was one of Jesus' three closest disciples. His biography of Jesus is found in the Bible's New Testament section, called the Gospel (Good News) according to John. John also wrote three letters to early followers of Jesus II JOHN, and III JOHN), and toward the end of his life he scribed a message which he claimed was sent by an angel containing the "Revelation of Jesus Christ."
Matthew - was a Jewish tax collector from the northern Israeli town of Capernaum, where Jesus spent most of his final, three years. Matthew was one of the closest disciples to Jesus. His biography of Jesus is also found in the Bible's New Testament section, called the Gospel (Good News) according to Matthew.
Paul - After gaining a reputation as one of the greatest persecutors of Christian followers to Jesus, Paul (formerly Saul), became one of the most outspoken proponents of Jesus. Paul traveled throughout Asia and Europe, eventually making statements about Jesus, directly to Caesar in Rome.
Peter - Was an uneducated man, a fisherman that through Jesus spent three years as an impertinent disciple and then became a powerful diplomat after witnessing Jesus rise from the dead.
John - In his biography about Jesus, he offered his perspective as one of Jesus' closest disciples. John liked to describe himself as the one whom Jesus loved.

THE BREAKDOWN OF THE BIBLE

"All Scripture is given by inspiration of God, and is profitable, for doctrine, for reproof, for correction, for instruction in righteousness" **(2 Timothy 3:16). Lets go over some of the facts about the Bible:**

1) Approximately 40 different men wrote the Scriptures.
2) They were from several different countries.
3) They lived at different times ranging from 1400BC through to 90AD.
4) The Scriptures were written in three languages Hebrew, Aramaic, and Greek.

These men were from different times and places, yet the Bible runs as smoothly as though they had all been in collaboration with each other. Hmmm, not possible when you look at the span of time it has taken to write the Bible. God by His Holy Spirit, moved all of these men to write the Scriptures, and that's the only way there could be such continuity, such a wonderful flow, how they all complement each other so beautifully. Therefore, the Scriptures in the Bible are His Words and inspired by God Himself.

How Is The Bible Made Up?

The Old Testament - This comprises in total of 39 books, and is filled with prophecy of the coming Messiah (Jesus Christ), including God's dealings with Israel and much, much, more.

The first five books are known as the **Pentateuch** or the "**Books of Moses"** and they are entitled:

Genesis – Creation, the fall, sin, how Israel came to be a nation and then came to be in Egypt.

Exodus – These Scriptures tell us about the deliverance of the people of Israel from slavery in Egypt.

Leviticus – These Scriptures explain the book of law.

Numbers – The wandering in the wilderness.

Deuteronomy – Scriptures explains the Israel People preparing to move into the Promised Land.

The next 12 books are historical books, they were written around 1400-450BC, and describe God's dealings with His people, Israel. These books are: **Joshua, Judges, Ruth, 1 Samuel, 2 Samuel, 1 Kings, 2 Kings, 1 Chronicles, 2 Chronicles, Ezra, Nehemiah & Esther.**

The following five books are poetic in nature, they describe in poetry and song God's greatness and dealings with men. These books are:

Job – The trust and suffering of a man who truly loved God.

Psalms – Songs of praise, also of instruction and guidance.

Proverbs – A guide to daily living, God's practical wisdom.

Ecclesiastes – How empty life is on earth without God.

Song of Solomon – A wonderful portrait of the love of God.

After this we move onto the prophets, as a prophet is someone who is commissioned by God to deliver His message to man. These books are known as the "Major Prophets" and were written from approximately 750 – 550BC and they are:

Isaiah, Jeremiah, Lamentations, Ezekiel & Daniel.

Moving further into the Old Testament, we find that the next 12 books are known as the "minor prophets" mainly due to them being shorter than the preceding five. These comprise the last 12 books of the Old Testament. They were written approximately 840 – 400BC:**Hosea, Joel, Amos, Obadiah, Jonah, Micah, Nahum, Habakkuk, Zephaniah, Haggai, Zechariah & Malachi.**

The previous information completes the Old Testament. Now, here is an interesting thought: "The New Testament is in the Old concealed. The Old Testament is in the New Revealed" All through the Old Testament, we can see parts where Jesus is prophesied; Isaiah is a wonderful example of this, as Isaiah spoke of the suffering of our Lord and Savior. David knew that a Savior would come. One thing that is crystal clear when we read the Old Testament is that there was great faith, these men spoke of things to come that would happen far into the future and far beyond their lifetime, but they still believed, that is true faith in God.

The New Testament

The New Testament is made up of 27 books in total showing the revealing of Jesus Christ, in it we find:

1) **The birth, life, death including the resurrection of our Lord and Savior Jesus Christ.**

2) **How to be saved.**

3) **The beginning of Christianity and the early church.**

4) **It is full of Wonderful instructions for Christian living.**

5) **The fulfillment of God's plan.**

The first four books of the New Testament are known as the Gospels and they are:

Matthew – The life of Christ written especially for the Jews, it reveals Jesus Christ as their long, a waited for Messiah.

Mark – This book reveals Jesus as the obedient servant of God; some say this was written to the Roman people, although it is not certain.

Luke – Emphasizes Christ's humanity, (100% man, 100% God). Again, supposedly this was written to the Greek world.

John – Here the deity of Jesus is stressed. It is sometimes surprising that the Gospels are in perfect harmony with each other, although written by four different men, from different backgrounds, and aimed at different audiences. Obviously, eye witnesses to Christ whilst working on this earth.

"*These are written, that ye might believe that Jesus if the Christ, the Son of God. And, that believing, ye might have life through his name*" **John 20:31 KJV.**

The next book of the New Testament is the book of Acts. Here we have the exciting accounts of the beginning and the growth of the Christian church. Next, we have the epistles or letters. These were written by the apostle Paul, you would notice that they are addressed to individuals and or churches; they were also for believers in general. These manuscripts tell every aspect of Christian faith, of how to lead a Godly life, also how a church should be run, and the responsibilities of a Christian.

There are 21 books, which are: **Romans, 1 Corinthians, 2 Corinthians, Galatians, Ephesians, Philippians, Colossians, 1 Thessalonians, 2 Thessalonians, 1 Timothy, 2 Timothy, Titus and Philemon.**

Then we move onto the General letters, which comprise eight books of the New Testament. Again, these books contain within their pages; instruction on how to live a victorious and faith filled Christian life: **Hebrews, James, 1 Peter, 2 Peter, 1 John, 2 John, 3 John, and Jude.**

Last but by no means least, the book of the end, this book is called **Revelation:** On first reading, this seems to be a bit of a scary book, but it is not, it is a message filled with hope for the future for believers in Christ. It tells us of the return of Christ, His reign, His glory, and the future state of believers, and unbelievers.

I trust in God that this information will help give you knowledge about the authenticity of the Bible and the facts, including the over-whelming truth in the Scriptures and how the Bible can give you guidance in the plan for ever persons life whilst on this earth. I know that once I had a better understanding of the breakdown in the Bible, it made sense to read all of the scriptures as I continually search to better my living for God's blessings in helping others around me.

CHAPTER SIX

Life Changing Scriptures

GOD'S INSPIRATION

How can the Word of God inspire us to receive a more fulfilled life in our walk with our Lord Jesus? I have constantly search the scriptures for daily inspirations and here are a few that helped me over the years. There have been times, when my faith was lacking, and I wanted to look towards my own drive and determination to make situations happen. I knew the only way forward was to seek God for His Will on my life and in all my personal and business endeavors. The following scriptures can help you when thoughts and feelings are running low. Everybody needs support at one time or another, and I feel these scripture can help you as they have helped me. "Thou hast also given me the shield of they salvation: and they right hand hath hold me up... Thou hast enlarged my steps under me, that my feet did not slip." **(Psalm 18:35-36)**

"Behold, the eye of the Lord is upon them that fear him, upon them that hope in his mercy; to deliver their soul from death, and to keep them alive in famine." **(Psalm 33:18-19)**

"I waited patiently for the Lord; and he inclined unto me, and heard my cry. He brought me up also out of an horrible pit, out of the miry clay, and set my feet upon a rock, and established my going," **(Psalm 40:1-2)**

"Trust in him at all times... pour out your heart before him: God is a refuge for us." **(Psalm 62:8)**

"Jesus said unto him, If though canst believe, all things are possible to him that believeth." **(Mark 9:23)**

"According as his divine power hath given unto us all things that pertain unto life and godliness, through the knowledge of him that hath called us to glory and virtue whereby are given unto us exceeding great and precious promises..." **(2 Peter 1:3-4)**

WHEN I'M AT WITS END:

*"Be still, and know that I am God: I will be exalted among the heathen, I will be exalted in the earth. The Lord of hosts is with us..."***Psalm 46:10-11** *"I will lift up mine eyes unto the hills from whence cometh my help. My help cometh from the Lord, which made heaven and earth. He will not suffer thy foot to be moved: he that keepeth thee will not slumber."*

Psalm 121:1-3 *"Thou wilt keep him in perfect peace, whose mind is stayed on thee: because he trusteth in thee."*

Isiah 26:3 *"It is of the Lord's mercies that we are not condemned, because his compassion's fail not. They are new every morning: great is they faithfulness."*

"The Lord also will be a refuge for the oppressed, a refuge in times of trouble." **(Psalm 9:9)**

"Wait on the Lord: be of good courage, and he shall strengthen thine heart: wait, I say on the Lord." **(Psalm 27:14)**

"The Lord will give strength unto his people; the Lord will bless his people with peace." **(Psalm 29:11)**

"For the Lord God is a sun and shield: the Lord will give grace and glory: no good thing will He withhold from them that walk uprightly." **(Psalm 84:11)**

"Thou openest thine hand, and satisfiest the desire of every living thing." **(Psalm 145:16)**

WHEN I NEED ASSURANCE THAT GOD IS THERE FOR ME:

"If My people, which are called by My name, shall humble themselves, and pray, and seek My face, and turn from their wicked ways; then will I hear from Heaven, and will forgive their sin, and will heal their land." **(2 Chronicles. 7:14)**

"But know that the Lord hath set apart him that is godly for himself: the Lord will hear when I call unto him." **(Psalm 4:3)**

"Evening, and morning, and at noon, will I pray, and cry aloud: and he shall hear my voice. He hath delivered my soul in peace from the battle that was against me..." **(Psalm 55: 17-18)**

"Ask and it shall be given you; seek, and ye shall find; knock and it shall be opened unto you: for every one that asketh receiveth; and he that seeketh findeth; and to him that knocketh it shall be opened." **(Matthew 7:7-8)**

"For verily I say unto you, that whosoever shall say unto this mountain, be thou removed, and be thou cast into the sea; and shall not doubt in his heart, but shall believe that those things which he saith shall come to pass; he shall have whatsoever he saith. Therefore I say unto you, what things soever ye desire, when ye pray, believe that ye receive them, and ye shall have them." **(Mark 11:23-24)**

"If ye abide in me, and my words abide in you, ye shall ask what ye will, and it shall be unto you." **(John 15:7)**

"If any of you lack wisdom, let him ask of God, that giveth to all men liberally, and upbraideth (scolds) not; and it shall be given him." **(James. 1:5)**

"And this is the confidence that we have in him, that, if we ask any thing according to his will, he heareth us: and if we know that he hears us. Whatsoever we ask, we know that we have the petitions that we desired of him." **(1 John 5:14-15)**

WHEN EVERYTHING GOES FROM BAD TO WORSE:

"And the Lord thy God will make thee plenteous in every work of thine hand... for the Lord will again rejoice over thee for good.... if thou shalt hearken unto the voice of the Lord they God, to keep his commandments and his statutes... and if though turn unto the Lord they God with all thine heart, and with all they soul." **Deut. 30:9-10**

"The Lord upholdeth all that fall, and raiseth up all those that be bowed down." **Psalm 145:14**

"...Blessed is the man that feareth the Lord, that delighteth greatly in his commandments... Wealth and riches shall be in his house: and his righteousness endureth forever. Unto the upright, there ariseth light in the darkness: he is gracious, and full of compassion, and righteous." **Psalm 112:1-4**

"...thus saith the Lord that created thee... I have called thee by thy name; thou art mine. When thou passest through the waters, I will be with thee; and through the rivers, they shall not overflow thee..." **Isiah 43:1-2**

WHEN I FEEL LIKE GIVING UP:

"And keep the charge of the Lord thy God, to walk in his ways, to keep his statutes, and his commandments, and his judgments, and his testimonies,... that thou mayest prosper in all that thou doest." **1 Kings 2:3**

"Cast thy burden upon the Lord, and he shall sustain thee: he shall never suffer the righteous to be moved." **Psalm 55:22**

"My flesh and my heart faileth: but God is the strength of my heart, and my portion forever." **Psalm 73:26**

WHEN GOD SEEMS FAR AWAY:

"The Lord is far from the wicked: but he heareth the prayer of the righteous." **Proverbs 15:29**

"For I the Lord thy God will hold thy right hand... Fear not; I will help thee... When the poor and needy seek water, and there is none... I the Lord will hear them..." **Isaiah 41:13,17**

"Behold, I have graven thee upon the palms of my hands." **Isiah 48:16**

"The Lord thy God in the midst of thee is mighty; he will save, he will rejoice over thee with joy..." **Zephaniah 3:17**

"Being confident of this very thing, that he which hath begun a good work in you will perform it until the day of Jesus Christ." **Phil. 1:6**

WHEN I NEED BOTH HELP & HOPE:

"If you need wisdom--if you want to know what God wants you to do--ask him, and he will gladly tell you." **James 1:5**

"This same God who takes care of me will supply all your needs from his glorious riches, which have been given to us in Christ Jesus." **Philippians 4:19**

God has given gifts to all of us. Are you called to help others? If so, do it with all the strength and energy that God supplies. **I Peter 4:10-11**

"Although the fig tree shall not blossom, neither shall fruit be in the vines; the labor of the olive shall fail, and the fields shall yield not meat; the flock shall be cut off from the fold, and there shall be no herd in the stalls: yet I will rejoice in the Lord, I will joy in the God of my salvation. The Lord God is my strength, and he will make my feet like hinds' feet, and he will make me to walk upon mine high places." **Habakkuk 3:17-19**

"The LORD taketh pleasure in them that fear him, in those that hope in his mercy." **Psalms 147:11**

"And hope maketh not ashamed; because the love of God is shed abroad in our hearts by the Holy Ghost, which is given unto us." **Romans 5:5**

"But sanctify the Lord God in your hearts: and be ready always to give an answer to every man that asketh you a reason of the hope that is in you with meekness and fear" **1 Peter 3:15**

WHEN I WORRY ABOUT THE FUTURE:

"The Lord is my shepherd; I shall not want. He maketh me to lie down in green pastures; he leadeth me beside the still waters. He restoreth my soul: he leadeth me in the paths of righteousness for his name's sake. Yea, thou I walk through the valley of the shadow of death, I will fear no evil: for though art with me thy rod and thy staff they comfort me. Thou preparest a table before me in the presence of mine enemies: thou anointest my head with oil; my cup runneth over. Surely goodness and mercy shall follow me all the days of my life: and I will dwell in the house of the Lord forever."

"The steps of a good man are ordered by the Lord: and he delighteth in his way. Though he fall, he shall not be utterly cast down: for the Lord upholdeth him with his hand." **Psalm 37:23-24**

"In the way of righteousness is life; and in the pathway thereof there is not death." **Proverbs 12:28**

"Give, and it shall be given unto you; good measure, pressed down, and shaken together, and running over, shall men give into your bosom. For with the same measure that ye mete (measure) withal it shall be measure to you again." **Luke 6:28**

"And this is the will of him that sent me, that every one which seeth the Son, and believeth on him, may have everlasting life: and I will raise him up at the last day." **John 6:40**

WHEN I FACE OPPOSITION:

"For thou hast girded me with strength unto the battle: thou has subdues under me those that rose up against me... He delivereth me from mine enemies... thou has delivered me from the violent man." **Psalm 18:39, 48**

"The angel of the Lord encampeth round about them that fear him, and delivereth them." **Psalms .34:7**

"When I cry unto thee, then shall mine enemies turn back: this I know; for God is for me" **Psalm 56:9**

WHEN I NEED TO KNOW RIGHT FROM WRONG:

"All the paths of the Lord are mercy and truth unto such as keep his covenant and his testimonies." **Psalm 25:10**

"Delight thyself also in the Lord; and he shall give thee the desires of the heart. Commit thy way unto the Lord; trust also in him; and he shall bring it to pass." **Psalm 37:4-5**

"My son, keep thy father's commandment, and forsake not the law of thy mother; bind them continually upon thine heart, and tie them about thy neck. When thou goest, it shall lead thee; when thou sleepest, it shall keep thee; and when thou awakest, it shall talk with thee." **Proverb 6:20-22**

WHEN I HAVE SINNED:

"Come now, and let us reason together, saith the Lord: though your sins be as scarlet, they shall be as white as snow; though they be red like crimson, they shall be as wool." **Isiah 1:18**

"I, even, I am he that blotteth out thy transgressions for mine own sake, and will not remember thy sins." **Isiah 43:25**

"Who is a God like unto thee, that pardoneth iniquity, because he delighteth in mercy: He will turn again, he will have compassion upon us; he will subdue our iniquities; and thou wilt cast all their sins into the depths of the sea." **Micah 7:18-19**

"If we confess our sins, he is faithful and just to forgive us our sins, and to cleanse us from all unrighteousness." **1 John 1:9**

WHEN I NEED STRENGTH:

"But let all those that put their trust in thee rejoice: let them ever shout for joy, because thou defendest them..." **Psalm 5:11**

"The Lord is my rock, and my fortress, and my deliverer; my God my strength, in whom I will trust..." **Psalm 18:2**

"God is our refuge and strength, a very present help in trouble, Therefore will not we fear, through the earth be removed, and though the mountains be carried into the midst of the sea." **Psalm 46:1-2**

"I can do all things through Christ which strengtheneth me." **Phil. 4:13**

"For which cause we faint not; but though our outward man perish, yet the inward man is renewed day by day."
2 Corinthians 4:16

"But the God of all grace, who hath called us unto his eternal glory by Christ Jesus, after that ye have suffered a while, make you perfect, stablish, strengthen, settle you." **1 Peter 5:10**

WHEN I AM IN TROUBLE:

"For the Lord thy God is a merciful God; he will not forsake thee..." **Deuteronomy 4:31**

"But thou, O Lord, are a shield for me; my glory, and the lifter up of min head." **Psalm 3:3**

"Yea, though I walk through valley of the shadow of death, I will fear no evil: for thou art with me; thy rod and they staff they comfort me." **Psalm 23:4**

"For in the time of trouble he shall hide me in his pavilion... he shall set me up upon a rock." **Psalm 27:5**

"Though I walk in the midst of trouble, thou wilt revive me: thou shalt stretch forth thine hand against the wrath of mine enemies, and thy right hand shall save me." **Psalm 138:7**

"Peace I leave with you, my peace I give unto you: not as the world giveth, give I unto you. Let not your heart be troubled, neither let it be afraid." **John 14:27**

"Blessed be God, even the Father of our Lord Jesus Christ, the Father of mercies, and the God of all comfort; who comforteth us in all our tribulation, that we may be able to comfort them which are in any trouble, by the comfort wherewith we ourselves are comforted of God." **2 Corinthians 1:3-4**

WHEN I AM FEARFUL:

"When thou liest down, thou shalt not be afraid: yea, thou shalt lie down, and thy sleep shall be sweet. Be not afraid of sudden fear, neither of the desolation of the wicked, when it cometh. For the Lord shall be thy confidence, and shall keep thy foot from being taken." **Proverbs 3:24-26**

"Fear thou not; for I am with thee: be not dismayed; for I am thy God: I will strengthen thee; yea I will help thee; yea, I will uphold thee with the right hand of my righteousness." **Isiah 41:10**

"For God hath not given us the spirit of fear; but of power, and of love, and of a sound mind." **2 Tim. 1:7**

WHEN I DON'T KNOW WHICH WAY TO TURN:

"And it shall come to pass, if thou shalt hearken diligently unto the voice of the Lord thy God, to observe and to do all his commandments... that the Lord thy God will see thee on high above all nations of the earth." **Deut. 28:1**

"If they obey and serve him, they shall spend their days in prosperity, and their years in pleasures." **Job 36:11**

"The eyes are ever toward the Lord; for he shall pluck my feet out of the net." **Psalm 25:15**

"In the fear of the Lord is strong confidence: and his children shall have a place of refuge. The fear of the Lord is a foundation of life..." **Proverbs 14:26-27**

WHEN NO ONE SEEMS TO CARE:

"Be strong and of good courage, fear not, nor be afraid of them: for the Lord thy god, he it is that doth go with thee; he will not fail thee, nor forsake thee." **Deut. 31:6**

"The eyes of the Lord are upon the righteous, and his ears are open unto their cry." **Psalm 34:15**

"Blessed be the Lord my strength my goodness, and my fortress; my high tower, and my deliverer; my shield, and he in whom I trust." **Psalm 144: 1-2**

"The Lord openeth the eyes of the blind; the Lord raiseth them that are bowed down: the Lord loveth the righteous: the Lord preserveth the strangers; he relieveth the fatherless and widow..." **Psalm 146:8-9**

"Blessed be the God and Father of our Lord Jesus Christ, who hath blessed us with all spiritual blessings in heavenly places in Christ." **Ephesians 1:3**

"And the peace of God, which passeth all understanding, shall keep your hearts and minds through Christ Jesus." **Philippians 4:7**

"For by one offering he hath perfected for ever them that are sanctified." **Hebrews 10:14**

CHAPTER SEVEN

MOVE MOUNTAINS WITH PRAYER

WHEN YOU PRAY, PRAY IN THE SPIRIT

"While our hands and head are at labor, our heart ought nevertheless rest in God. God is a Spirit. He dwells in the Spirit, works in the Spirit, prays in the Spirit, and does everything in the Spirit; for remember we also are Spirits, and therefore are created in the Image of God. When we present ourselves to God, we need to stand before him as a naked Spirit in Simplicity and Purity so that we can communicate to Him in the Spirit."

Does Prayer Alter the Outcome of Our Daily Circumstances?

We know that God works all things together after His own will **(Ephesians. 1:11)**, so that whether we pray or not God's purposes will be accomplished. The point is, God has chosen in His plan to use our prayers and for this reason we have many promises from God that says prayer does accomplish things. Read: **(James 5:13-16**). Therefore, the answer is a "yes" prayer does change the outcome of things. God does intervene based on prayer, but again, this is because He has chosen to use our prayers to accomplish His purposes for our lives whilst we are on this earth. In addition, prayer is a means of manifesting our faith and dependence on Him, and so of bringing glory to our Almighty God. One of the main purposes for praying is to have an impact on our own hearts and lives as God uses it to conform us to His will and transform us into His character. It's a place of fellowship and intimacy, of growth and transformation, of learning His will as one asks, seeks, and knocks at the door of God's heart, etc.

DO PEOPLE GET HEALED THROUGH PRAYER?

There is no doubt that prayers are answered and sometimes infrequently. However, there is no guarantee that a particular condition will be miraculously healed through prayer or by following some recommendations in the Scriptures such as fasting and laying-on-of-hands. Only God seems to know why He heals some people, but not others - or to what extent faith is involved. When an investigative reporters followed some of those who initially professed to have been healed in attending miracle crusades it turned out that only days or weeks later, every one was still afflicted with the same conditions. Worse still specific terminal cases, where the entire congregation joined in prayer, had died. I have heard of a number of patients who confessed to having had a miracle healing, but after the initial euphoria had worn off, every single one still suffered from the same affliction and needed therapy for there illness. (God can also indirectly heal or cure you by giving special gifts to talented surgeons and doctors were they are obligated through God from your prayer.) In some cases, were laying-on-of-hands and prayers have been used, blood tests showed that a particular disease-causing organism had disappeared with no repercussions. It appears that when prayers are answered for any particular problem, God seems to change the circumstances, or opens doors, but He may not necessarily take away the afflictions or problems Himself. Sick people still seem to have to go through any possible ordeal the hard way trying to get better, and only if nothing earthly is capable of remedying the situation, then sometimes prayers are answered literally. Miracles can happen, or perhaps they are answered whenever they happen to suit God's particular purpose.

ANSWERS TO PRAYER IN FAITH

"Have faith in God. Truly I tell you, if you say to this mountain, 'be taken up and thrown into the sea,' and if you do not doubt in your heart, but believe that what you say will come to pass, it will be done for you. So I tell you, whatever you ask for in prayer, believe that you have received it, and it will be yours." **(Mark 11:22-24)**

"For truly I tell you, if you have faith the size of a mustard seed, you will say to this mountain, 'Move from here to there,' and it will move; and nothing will be impossible for you." **(Matthew 17:20)**

"If you abide in me, and my words abide in you, ask for whatever you wish, and it will be done for you." **(John 15:7)**

"Is there anyone among you who, if your child asks for bread, will give a stone? Or if the child asks for a fish, will give a snake? If you then, who are evil, know how to give good gifts to your children, how much more will your Father in heaven given good things to those who ask him." **(Matthew 7:9-11)**

PRAYING WITH CONFIDENCE

Disappointment has a way of turning prayers into silence. It can be hard to pray when you are bitter and angry toward people you believe are ruining your life. It can be even harder to pray when you feel that God Himself has let you down. God understands our feelings. Yet, He has made a way for us to come with confidence to His throne of grace.*" he that cometh to God must believe that he is, and that he is a rewarder of them that diligently seek Him."* **(Hebrews 11:6)**

"Let all bitterness and wrath, and anger, and clamour, and evil speaking, be put away from you, with all malice: And be ye kind one to another, tenderhearted, forgiving one another, even as God for Christ's sake hath forgiven you." **(Ephesians 4:31-32)**

DO YOU PRAY ENOUGH?

When it comes to prayer, would you respond?

- That you do not pray enough.
- You do not really know how to pray?
- I do not know if praying really works.

I have found such answers common with the people that I have met on a daily basis. While a few speak glowingly of the ease in which they slip in and out of the conversations that they have with God. Many of the people that I have spoken with seem to view prayer, as a struggle.

As it can sometimes be easier depending on the prayer, or it can be extremely difficult when they think it could be an embarrassing situation, or a life changing decision. It is understandable that prayer would not always come easy. It is not just emotion stress people experience when trying to pray, it can also be an expression of faith that is often weak and can be classes as spiritual warfare, were you feel that you are fighting for contested ground. It is a reflection in lack of confidence and ignorance in a relationship with God. Early in our Christian walk, we prayed with high expectations.

We automatically assume that God will give us the deepest desires of our heart and through prayer, we will experience; the closeness and happiness that we long for with our God, we also believe that we will rise above any situation. Then we ask God for something important to us and we do not get it. We assure ailing friends that we are praying for their recovery, but they do not get better.

We pray in the presence of our family, for a solution to problems that are affecting them, only to be left waiting for months and months while God seems to ignore us. We plead earnestly and often for our loved ones' spiritual restoration, but they still remain distant from God. Slowly, disappointment forms. We lose our enthusiasm for prayer and soon we are praying only at mealtimes and as brief as possible. We go through a phase when we will not bring anything we really care about to the Lord, because we cannot take another rejection. We stop communicating with God. Think a minute about your prayer relationship with God. If you have stopped growing in prayer, is it because of honest disappointment?

- **Disappointment with God.**

"I asked and believed that God was going to heal my mother, but she lost her fight with cancer anyway."

- **Disappointment with others.**

"I have a hard time praying when I am so angry with people who are ruining my life."

- **Disappointment with ourselves.**

"I've wanted to pray, but I did not know what to say to God. I have the best of intentions and will try harder."

It takes faith and courage to work through a disrupted human relationship. It is the same in our relationship with God. The first step is to admit the problem. Then we must work past the disappointment and regain our confidence in God. I have been through this issues myself in the past as God did not answer all of my prayers, and I am sure God had his reasons, through His plans for you and other.

BE HONEST WHEN PRAYING

God loves us to talk honestly with Him. Realism is at the heart of His own character. He hates darkness and deception. Darkness is the domain of His enemy. Therefore, to be confident in prayer is to learn to be honest about what is in our hearts. God can handle our complaints, our foolishness, our fears, and our failures. God will never be surprised or threatened by our anger, our confusion, or our childlike pleading. What displeases God are the cheap lies of flattery, ritual praise, insincere words repeated over and over without regret for what is coming from your mouth, that does not come from your heart and soul. We need to put away our practices of fearful praying; prayers filled lies are as unacceptable to God, as lies would to you from somebody very close like your husband and or wife. That is why, in order to enter the God's grace and begin to pray with confidence, we must learn to tell the truth when we pray. To do this, we have to spend time in evaluation and confession of sin. We must tell God how we really feel about Him, about ourselves, about our problems with people, and about our needs, frustrations, desires, and painful memories. We must also be honest about our desire to make His Will our own. When we want to know the truth about ourselves, God will already know. We have to share these feeling with Him, so that He can help us see a way through our heart ache. This will all be based on us wanting to talk further with Him. Just think back when you were younger and how at times it was difficult share your deepest, personal feeling with your loved ones. I know, when I was young, I also felt this way in talking, with my mum and dad thinking: "How can they understand me?" Well it can be somewhat similar when trying and or wanting to converse with our Heavenly Father.

"O LORD, You have searched me and known me" **(Psalms. 139:1)**.

"For I know the plans I have for you, "declares the Lord," plans to prosper you and not to harm you, plans to give you hope and a future. Then you will call upon me and come and pray to me, and I will listen to you." **(Jeremiah 29: 11-12).**

"The LORD searches all hearts and understands all the intent of the thoughts" **(1 Chronicles. 28:9).**

Praying when combined with Scriptures, enables us to see what is really going on inside. The Bible shows us our deep-seated feelings and true motives. It takes us into the nooks and crannies where we hide old grudges and secret hatreds and bitter resentments. Through honest prayer we can bring these things to the surface, see them for what they really are, and ask God to help us deal with them and from this, we can be confident. If we ask God to show us our hearts, He will do it. God may do this over a period of time with you as he did with me when I found it extremely hard to forgive my first wife and for the guilt in leaving my children with her in England. In God's own way, the Lord will pull back the curtains of denial and repression and show us ourselves. God may bring out an old hurt to mend so that we can deal with and forget. God might remind us of a promise we have not kept, or a debt we have not paid in full. God may let us feel the hurt we gave to someone else, perhaps many years ago, and tell us to make it right. He may even get us to put misunderstandings and mistakes to right for someone. Having truth in your heart is a wonderful, liberating gift, and it comes through being honest with God in prayer.

Praying and reading God's Scriptures can also reveal the positive blessings in our lives that God is working and achieving for us, all the time. God shows us His grace and goodness, by filling us with the Holy Spirit and through this God will also help us grow through adversity, sustain us through difficult circumstances, and by giving us ways to escape temptation. Most importantly, grant us with His peace with no stress, no worries, no fear, just wonderful peace within us. I was talking to my wife Angela regarding my prayer's and conversations with God and how He does and sometimes doesn't, provide me with all the right answers, at the time when I feel that they are needed most. My wife then said to me that she feels God rarely talks to her. I said; "what? God does talk to you." Sometimes you may thing about something and sub-consciously involve God in your conversation. My wife replied: "Yes that has happened." Maybe days, months or even years later, God replies by sending your request in the form of a person that gives you that answer. My wife replied: "Now that I am thinking about it, yes God has done things that way." God can deal with prayer and your concerns in different forms. I told Angela that I remember her telling me, that she prayed constantly, for month after month, that could of ending up in years, to meet her ideal sole mate. She relied; yes, but I had confidence that one day, God will find the ideal person to share her life with, that also included God in that relationship." I then replied by saying: That I too was praying for a sole mate and God brought us together." Whilst I was thinking about another, way in which to explain that God listens to all of us. God revealed to me that it sometimes would take time, as sometimes we may not be at the right place and or at the right precise moment in our lives for our request to be fulfilled. God wanted us both to be together, but it was when the moment was right.

It was more important that he got us into a position suitable for us both to be joined together, whereby we would find His blessing. I felt that God answered both our prayers that way, so both of us can learn from God, in finding how we both can become the ideal sole mate for each other. Whether God talks to you directly or indirectly, He listens. God will give you a solution to your issues personally, or He will send his decision with a messenger. We can also struggle with God, in the way of complaints regarding our long awaited prayers. As many of us have accepted society's idea that struggle and love do not go together. We assume that a relationship is good only as long as there is peace and harmony. The fact remains that relationships struggle when God is out of the triangular framework. The triangle should be as one, with God at the top, with the Husband and wife at the same level below, all working together in harmony. Sometimes finding the courage to discuss our struggles takes risks and confrontation, that will normally end-up strengthening and deepen all relationships. The same is true in our relationship with God. Like Jacob at Bethel, we do well to wrestle with God once-in-a-while. It can bring us His blessing. **(Gen. 32:24-32).** One of the plans that the believer through Jesus Christ has, is to become one (in heart and agreement) with God. When we come to Him in prayer, we need to be honest with ourselves, about whether our desires are His desires, whether our will is His will, whether our requests would be His requests. We can never share in His complete understanding of all things, but as we pray for the daily needs of life, for our spouse and children and friends, for healing, or employment and guidance. We can do so with the same attitude of heart Jesus had in mind when He taught His disciples to pray to the Father.

"Your will be done on earth as it is in heaven" **(Matthew. 6:10).**

Jesus Himself expressed that same attitude a few hours before His death. He concluded an agonizing prayer session in Gethsemane, when He even asked the Father to let Him avoid the cross by saying: *"Nevertheless not My will, but Yours, be done"* **(Luke 22:42)**. This surrender, after an intense honest struggle, kept Him in a spirit of oneness with His Father. We may have questions about praying, "Your will be done." Does that mean we are telling God that we are secretly giving up on what we just prayed about? Are we telling God that our pray was offered without the true conviction that we thought was right and that God should answer it how He sees fit? What does 'Thy will be done' means? It means:

"Thou understandest my prayer better than I understand it myself." **(Romans. 8:26.)**

"Thou knowest most whether I need hunger or bread. Whatever may come, I will still say, Yes, dear Lord" **(Matthew. 15:27)**.

When we pray, "Your will be done," we are choosing to be at one with God. We are saying to Him, what Jesus said to His disciples: *"My food is to do the will of Him who sent Me"* **(John 4:34.)**

In actual effect, we are echoing the Lord's Prayer in Gethsemane. Whether or not He gives us bread, or a job, or a sole mate or a child, His will done His way is best.

JESUS TELLS US HOW TO PRAY

*1 And it came to pass, that, as he was praying in a certain
place, when he ceased, one of his disciples said unto him,
Lord, teach us to pray, as John also taught his disciples.
2 And he said unto them, When ye pray, say, Our Father
which art in heaven, Hallowed be thy name. Thy kingdom
come. Thy will be done, as in heaven, so in earth.
3 Give us day by day our daily bread.
4 And forgive us our sins; for we also forgive every one that
is indebted to us. And lead us not into temptation; but
deliver us from evil.
5 And he said unto them, Which of you shall have a friend,
and shall go unto him at midnight, and say unto him,
Friend, lend me three loaves;
6 For a friend of mine in his journey is come to me, and I
have nothing to set before him?
7 And he from within shall answer and say, Trouble me not:
the door is now shut, and my children are with me in bed; I
cannot rise and give thee.
8 I say unto you, Though he will not rise and give him,
because he is his friend, yet because of his importunity he
will rise and give him as many as he needeth.
9 And I say unto you, Ask, and it shall be given you; seek,
and ye shall find; knock, and it shall be opened unto you.
10 For every one that asketh receiveth; and he that seeketh
findeth; and to him that knocketh it shall be opened".*

(Luke 11: 1-10.)

In the Bible, it also gives us other examples of how to pray:

[54] *And it was so, that when Solomon had made an end of praying all this prayer and supplication unto the LORD, he arose from before the altar of the LORD, from kneeling on his knees with his hands spread up to heaven.* **(1 Kings 8:54)**

[25] *And when ye stand praying, forgive, if ye have ought against any: that your Father also which is in heaven may forgive you your trespasses.* **(Mark 11:25)**

[5] *And when thou prayest, thou shalt not be as the hypocrites are:*
for they love to pray standing in the synagogues and in the
corners of the streets, that they may be seen of men. Verily I say
unto you, They have their reward. [6] *But thou, when thou prayest,*
enter into thy closet, and when thou hast shut thy door, pray to
thy Father which is in secret; and thy Father which seeth in
secret shall reward thee openly. [7] *But when ye pray, use not vain*
repetitions, as the heathen do: for they think that they shall be
heard for their much speaking. [8] *Be not ye therefore like unto*
them: for your Father knoweth what things ye have need of,
before ye ask him. **(Matthew 6: 5-8)**

[29] *The LORD is far from the wicked: but he heareth the prayer of the righteous.* **(Proverbs 15:29)**

LIVING A CHRISTIAN LIFE

Believe in the scriptures of the New Testament that through Jesus, you have received eternal life. **(1 John 5:10-13.)** Remember that you are now a living testimony of the saving power of the Lord Jesus Christ and that the life of Christ is in you, as a believer. You must love God and all of His people, also you must love God with all your heart, soul, mind and strength according to **Mark 12:30 -31**. Ask the Lord to help and guide you to love more and more.

1 Thessalonians 3:12 ***"And the Lord make you to increase and abound in love one toward another, and toward all men, even as we do toward you:"***

Consistently read and study your Bible, by memorizing portions that are helpful to you and give special attention to the promises of God. Meditate on these and they will be food for your soul.

1 Peter 2:2. ***"As newborn babes, desire the sincere milk of the word, that ye may grow thereby."***

Remember that the Word of God is the light to your pathway.

Psalms 119:105 ***"Thy word is a lamp unto my feet, and a light unto my path." It is the weapon of our warfare, Ephesians 6:17, "And take ... the sword of the Spirit, which is the word of God."***

Pray daily to your heavenly Father, in the name of the Lord Jesus Christ. Thank Him for all things that He has and is doing for you, including those that you hear testimonials from.

Ephesians 5:20: ***"Giving thanks always for all things unto God and the Father in the name of our Lord Jesus Christ."***

Give praise to God for His blessings upon you and ask God to give you victory over sin and weakness of the flesh.

1 John 1:9: ***"If we confess our sins, he is faithful and just to forgive us our sins, and to cleanse us from all unrighteousness."***

Pray for the needs of others while you are praying for your own needs, remember that your prayer when you pray, talk to God from your heart and in your own words, as this will keep you spiritually strong. Confess the Lord Jesus Christ as your personal Savior as often as you can and continue confessing Christ to others around you.

Matthew 10:32. ***"Whosoever therefore shall confess me before men, him will I confess also before my Father which is in heaven."***

Use every opportunity you have to tell others what the Lord Jesus Christ has done in your life. Avoid temptations at all times, as the Bible tells us that they will come.

Psalms 1:1 "***Blessed is the man that walketh not in the counsel of the ungodly, nor standeth in the way of sinners, nor sitteth in the seat of the scornful."***

When temptations arise, remember that God has promised a way of escape for those who faithfully serve and obey Him through His words and commandments: **1 Corinthians 10:13,** ***"There hath no temptation taken you but such as is common to man: but God is faithful, who will not suffer you to be tempted above that ye are able; but will with the temptation also make a way to escape, that ye may be able to bear it."***

Pray that the Lord will help you avoid temptation: **Matthew 6:13** ***"And lead us not into temptation, but deliver us from evil: For thine is the kingdom, and the power, and the glory, for ever. Amen."***

Witness to others about the Lord Jesus Christ: **Acts 1:8** ***"But ye shall receive power, after that the Holy Ghost is come upon you: and ye shall be witnesses unto me both in Jerusalem, and in all Judaea, and in Samaria, and unto the uttermost part of the earth."***

Many today do not know Jesus Christ as their personal savior. Who will tell them? **Romans 10:13-14** ***"For whosoever shall call upon the name of the Lord shall be saved. How then shall they call on him in whom they have not believed? and how shall they believe in him of whom they have not heard? and how shall they hear without a preacher?"***

The believer's greatest joy is the privilege of telling the good news of the Gospel to every creature.

Witnessing for Christ is not only a blessed privilege, but also a divine command: **Matthew 4:19:** ***"And he saith unto them, Follow me, and I will make you fishers of men."***

Serve the Lord with gladness: **Psalms 100:2**: ***"Serve the LORD with gladness: come before his presence with singing."***

God has a regular ministry for every believer in Him: **(Read 1 Corinthians 12:12-21.)**

Go to God's church regularly: **Hebrews 10:25**. ***"Not forsaking the assembling of ourselves together, as the manner of some is; but exhorting one another: and so much the more, as ye see the day approaching."***

Invest your time, talents and money for eternity: **Colossians 3:1-3.** ***"If ye then be risen with Christ, seek those things which are above, where Christ sitteth on the right hand of God. Set your affection on things above, not on things on the earth. For ye are dead, and your life is hid with Christ in God."***

Always stand firm by the Word of God, read: **(Ephesians 6:10-18)**.

Beware of false teachers and false doctrines: **2 Peter 2:1-3** ***"But there were false prophets also among the people, even as there shall be false teachers among you, who privily shall bring in damnable heresies, even denying the Lord that bought them, and bring upon themselves swift destruction. And many shall follow their pernicious ways; by reason of whom the way of truth shall be evil spoken of. And through covetousness shall they with feigned words make merchandise of you: whose judgment now of a long time lingereth not, and their damnation slumbereth not."***

Test everything by the Word of God, not by experience: **Isaiah 8:20.** ***"To the law and to the testimony: if they speak not according to this word, it is because there is no light in them."***

Remember that God has promised the victory to those who honor Him and His Holy Word:

1Corinthians 15:58 ***"Therefore, my beloved brethren, be ye stedfast, unmoveable, always abounding in the work of the Lord, forasmuch as ye know that your labour is not in vain in the Lord."***

The Bible says that God designs the circumstances of our lives in a way that will prompt us to look for Him. For those who do reach out for Him, the Scriptures also say that He is close enough to be found. According to the apostle Paul, God is a Spirit in whom "we live, move, and have our being."

ACTS 17: 26-28: *"And hath made of one blood all nations of men for to dwell on all the face of the earth, and hath determined the times before appointed, and the bounds of their habitation; That they should seek the Lord, if haply they might feel after him, and find him, though he be not far from every one of us: For in him we live, and move, and have our being; as certain also of your own poets have said, For we are also his offspring."*

The Bible makes it clear, that we must reach out for God on His terms rather than our own. He promises to be found, not by just anyone, but by those who admit their own need and are willing to trust Him rather than themselves. When reading God's Written Words, we need to read the Bible scriptures correctly whereby we are not misinterpretation the Word of God. For God's Written Word's will build an intimate relationship with our Heavenly Father, which in-turn will make our love for God's Word grow in all of us. In John 6:63, Jesus Christ emphasized how important God's Written Word are: ***"It is the Spirit who gives life; the flesh profits nothing. The words that I speak to you are spirit, and they are life."***

Jesus tells us that the Holy Spirit imparts life to us and God's Word is spirit and life. The Word of God is not dead, or lifeless. Therefore, our interpretations and theological theories about the Word of God are dead and lifeless, but true interpretations of the Word are not. The Word of God is living and active in its original "God-intended meaning." In Matthew 4:4, Jesus said that God's Word is more important to us than even food: ***"But He answered and said, 'It is written, "Man shall not live by bread alone, but by every word that proceeds from the mouth of God."***

Christians should not worship the cover, paper and ink of the Bible, as they should feel and have *awe,* or *reverence* for the Words of God recorded in the Bible. In Ezra 9:4: "***Then were assembled unto me every one that trembled at the words of the God of Israel, because of the transgression of those that had been carried away; and I sat astonied until the evening sacrifice."*** Ezra 10:3***: "Now therefore let us make a covenant with our God to put away all the wives, and such as are born of them, according to the counsel of my lord, and of those that tremble at the commandment of our God; and let it be done according to the law."***

Isaiah 66:2-5 refers to *trembling* in relation to the Word of God. Isaiah 66:2 records that the Lord said: ***"...But on this one will I look: on him who is poor and of a contrite spirit, and who trembles at My word."*** To have trembles means to have awe, or reverence in relation to the Word of God and we reverence His Word, because He has spoken it.

In the Bible it gives an example of standing with awe of God's Word: Psalm 119:161-162 ***"...but my heart stands in awe of Your word. I rejoice at Your word as one who finds great treasure."***

In loving God's Words the Psalmist wrote in Psalms 19:119 and 167, that he *loved* the testimonies of God's Word: "***119: Thou puttest away all the wicked of the earth like dross: therefore I love thy testimonies."*** Verse 67***: "My soul hath kept thy testimonies; and I love them exceedingly."***

In **Psalm 119: 47, 48 and 127**, God led the Psalm-writer to declare he *loved* God's commandments. In 119:159, the writer says he *loved* the precepts of God's Word. ***"Precepts"*** here the Psalmist refers to the responsibilities that God places on His people.

Psalms 119: 47: *And I will delight myself in thy commandments, which I have loved.* 48: *My hands also will I lift up unto thy commandments, which I have loved; and I will meditate in thy statutes.* 127: *Therefore I love thy commandments above gold; yea, above fine gold.* 159: *Consider how I love thy precepts: quicken me, O LORD, according to thy lovingkindness.*

God's intention of the Bible is not to treat it as some form of lucky charm to carry around with you. In addition, we should not bow down and worship the Bible, but we should love the Word of God, as recorded in the Bible. Psalm 119:132 refer to loving God's Name. "***Psalms 119:132: Look thou upon me, and be merciful unto me, as thou usest to do unto those that love thy name.***"

In John 17:17, Jesus said that God's Word is *absolutely true*: ***"...Your Word is truth."*** Psalm 33:4 reveals God's Word is *absolutely right*. Matthew 24:35 declares: ***"Heaven and earth will pass away, but My words will by no means pass away."***

In John 14:23, Jesus said that if we love Him, we would then obey His Word: "***Jesus answered and said unto him, If a man love me, he will keep my words: and my Father will love him, and we will come unto him, and make our abode with him.***"

Psalm 119:9-11 reveals one of the keys to victory in our walk with God, is knowing and obeying His Word and its commandments: ***"How can a young man cleanse his way? By taking heed according to Your word. With my whole heart I have sought You; oh, let me not wander from Your commandments! Your word I have hidden in my heart, that I might not sin against You."***

Because Jesus Christ is God, (God The **Father**, The **Son** & Holy **Spirit**.) He is the perfect interpreter of the Bible. He is in perfect union with God the Father and God the Holy Spirit, as we can see how the Father and the Holy Spirit interpret the written Word of God in observing how Christ interpreted it. Here are Christ's principles for interpreting the written Word of God:

Jesus did not interpret verses contrary to other verses as shown in Matthew 4:5-6 that reveals; Jesus and Satan interpreted the Bible through different methods. These verses record Satan interpreted passages of Scripture in isolation from other verses and passages on the same or related topics: ***"Then the devil took Him up into the holy city, set Him on the pinnacle of the temple, and said to Him, 'If You are the Son of God, throw yourself down. For it is written: "He shall give His angels charge over you, and 'In their hands they shall bear you up, lest you dash your foot against a stone.'"***

Satan implied **Psalm 91:11-12** contained a promise that God the Father would allow His power to be used for showing-off purposes. Satan was able to suggest this false interpretation because he took this verse in isolation from other verses of Scripture.

However, Jesus Christ showed all verses must be interpreted in agreement with the meaning of other verses of Scriptures, which can relate to the same topic. He did this by answering Satan's false interpretation of **Psalm 91:11-12** with **Deuteronomy 6:16**. Matthew 4:7 records:

"Jesus said to him, 'It is written again, "You shall not tempt the Lord your God.'" By quoting **Deuteronomy 6:16**, Jesus taught that **Psalm 91:11-12** cannot be taken to mean that we can force God to use His power just for show.

If Satan can wrongly interpret verses of Scripture by taking them in isolation, so can we as humans. In this example, the Lord Jesus revealed He regards two methods of interpreting verses from the Scriptures correctly, which are:

1. Not taking any verse in isolation.
2. Making sure that one's interpretation of the verses agree with the wording of other verses on the same topic in other parts of the Bible.

We can only find the full true meaning to a particular matter of God's Words by studying all of His commands and instructions. If we leave out one verse of the topic, we can then make great errors through God's written Words. In addition, we need to consider any exceptions, which God makes to these commands and instructions, as they need to be read together.

For us to be filled with the Holy Spirit like Jesus, we must follow His example in interpreting and applying verses of Scripture to our lives in ways, which are in agreement with other verses on the same topic. A sign that believers are truly being filled with the Holy Spirit is; when we apply God's general commands to more specific, practical, life situations that will turn from and repent of any disobedience to His specifically applied commands.

Jesus disapproved of man-made rules through the Bible Scriptures were misinterpretation was being used as shown in **Mark 7:1-8**, Jesus Christ revealed that it is a sin to make rules, or commands for believers which are:

Contrary to other Biblical verses on the same topic and/or not specifically commanded in the Bible for believers under the relevant covenant(s), through which the believers are living.

For example, in **Mark 7:1-8**, Jesus rebuked many, or all of the scribes and Pharisees for teachings as commands of God the man-made religious traditions, that they must wash their hands in a special way before eating and that after coming from the market place they must wash. There are no specific, or broad Biblical commands, or teachings, which support these above religious traditions.

Mark 7:1-8: "***Then came together unto him the Pharisees, and certain of the scribes, which came from Jerusalem. And when they saw some of his disciples eat bread with defiled, that is to say, with unwashen, hands, they found fault. For the Pharisees, and all the Jews, except they wash their hands oft, eat not, holding the tradition of the elders. And when they come from the market, except they wash, they eat not. And many other things there be, which they have received to hold, as the washing of cups, and pots, brasen vessels, and of tables. Then the Pharisees and scribes asked him, Why walk not thy disciples according to the tradition of the elders, but eat bread with unwashen hands? He answered and said unto them, Well hath Esaias prophesied of you hypocrites, as it is written, This people honoureth me with their lips, but their heart is far from me. Howbeit in vain do they worship me, teaching for doctrines the commandments of men. For laying aside the commandment of God, ye hold the tradition of men, as the washing of pots and cups: and many other such like things ye do.***"

It is possible the Pharisees had misinterpreted the symbolic expressions about clean hands in **Psalm: 18:20, 18:24, 24:3-4** and **Job: 17:9**, and or had sinfully broadened the specific command of God, that related to Israelite priests under the Mosaic Covenant of washing their hands and feet, at the laver of bronze before entering the Tabernacle (see **Exodus 30:18-21**), to apply to Israelites who were not priests and to washing other things besides hands and feet. **Psalm 18:20, 18:24, 24:3-4** and **Job 17:9** refer to clean hands as being *symbols* of our attitudes and actions, being pure and free of guilt. In **Deuteronomy 21:6**, the washed hands of the city's elders were symbols of their innocence. **James 4:8** links the symbolic phrase ***"Cleanse your hands"*** to having a pure heart.

Note in Mark 7:4, Mark accused many for wrongly teaching many of their other religious traditions as commands of God. Mark records ***"there are many other things which they have received and hold."***

It is very easy to fall into the false methods of interpreting Scripture which Jesus rebuked in **Mark 7:1-8**. For example, someone can wrongly interpret Peter's words in **1 Peter 3:3-4** to mean it is sinful to wear gold wedding rings, gold watches, or gold earrings. However, note **Exodus 3:22, 28:15-21, 39:8-14,** and **Proverbs 25:12** reveal that God approves of believers wearing such gold ornaments.

Therefore, **1 Peter 3:3-4** is instead, teaching that a woman should place a higher priority on having a good heart and spirit, then on her outward appearance. There are numerous and even popular methods of interpreting the written Word of God, which are contrary to the principles Jesus used. Jesus taught that if the Scriptures contain God-approved specific exceptions to God's broad commands, we could then obey the exception without being guilty of breaking the broader command. These exceptions can come in the form of *more specific commands,* or they can be *historical Biblical examples*.

In **Matthew 12:3-4**, Jesus gave an *historical Biblical example* in which an exception to a broad command of God was permitted by God, without the persons involved becoming guilty before Him. Christ was referring to the exception found in **1 Samuel 21:1-6**. In this latter passage and throughout the rest of the Bible, it does not say David and his men sinned in eating the consecrated bread, which the High Priest gave them.

God permitted this exception because of the great hunger of David and his men. They were hiding from Saul's soldiers who desired to kill them. God wanted David to live and later be king. However, observe that when David tried to make his own exceptions to God's commands against adultery and murder and against moving the Ark of the Covenant by anyone other than the Levites, God did not approve of these exceptions. The Bible records David sinned greatly in these matters (**2 Samuel 6:1-9, 11:1-12:14** and **1 Chronicles 13:1-12**).

Nowhere in the Bible does it justify us in making our own exceptions to God's commands. To do so is to become like the lawless hypocritical Pharisees did in **Matthew 15:3-9** and **Mark 7:9-13**.

How the Apostles and Hebrews' author interpreted the Scriptures.

A detailed study of the way the Apostles Paul, Peter, James, John, Jude, and the writer of the Book of Hebrews quoted and interpreted verses from the Old Testament is extremely helpful in learning how to interpret Bible verses correctly. These Biblical authors interpreted various Old Testament verses as:

Prophecies - Examples of these are found in Acts 2:17-21, 2:25-28, 2:34-35, 3:22-23, 3:25, 4:11, 4:25-26, 8:32-33, 13:33-35, 15:16-17, 28:26-27, Romans 9:25, 9:27-28, 9:29, 9:33, 11:8, 11:9-10, 11:26-27, 14:11, 15:3, 15:9-12, 15:21, 1 Corinthians 2:9, 15:54-55, 2 Corinthians 6:2, 6:18, Galatians 3:8, 3:16, Ephesians 4:8, Hebrews 1:5, 1:6, 1:8-9, 1:10-12, 1:13, 5:5, 5:6, 7:17, 7:21, 8:8-12, 10:16-17, 12:26, 1 Peter 2:6, 2:7-8, 2:22, Revelation 2:27 and 3:7.

Old Testament teachings which are generally applied to the New Covenant times - Examples of these are seen in Acts 7:49-50, Romans 1:17, 3:10-18, 9:15, 10:5-8, 10:11, 10:13, 10:15, 1 Corinthians 3:19-20, 2 Corinthians 9:9, Galatians 3:10, 3:11, 3:12, Hebrews 2:6-8, 3:7-11, 3:15, 4:7, 9:20, 10:5-7, 10:37-38, 12:5-6, 13:5, 13:6, James 4:6, 1 Peter 1:24-25, 3:10-12, 4:18 and 5:5.

Old Testament teachings reapplied to more specific contexts under the New Covenant - For example see 1 Corinthians 10:26 and 10:28 which quote Psalm 24:1 and 1 Corinthians 15:32 which quotes Isaiah 22:13. Psalm 24:1 says: ***"The earth is the Lord's, and all its fullness, the world and those who dwell therein."*** But note 1 Corinthians 10:26 and 10:28 relate the teachings of the above verse to the more specific matter of whether to eat meat which had been sacrificed to idols.

Historical examples - Which have general relevance also to New Covenant believers. See Acts: 13:22, 4:3, 4:22, 9:12, 9:13, 9:17, 11:3, 11:4, 1 Corinthians 10:7, Galatians 3:6, Hebrews 4:4, 12:20 and 12:21. (These verses show how wrong is the common idea that historical Biblical books like Genesis, 1 Samuel, 1 Kings, Acts and so on can never be used for determining Biblical doctrine. As long as historical events in the Bible are interpreted in ways not contrary to other verses on the same topic, these events can be used as a part of determining what the Bible teaches.)

Historical examples reapplied to new specific New Covenant contexts - For example, read 2 Corinthians 4:13 which quotes Psalm 116:10, 2 Corinthians 8:15 which uses Exodus 16:18 and Galatians 4:30 which quotes Genesis 21:10-12.

Broad Old Testament commands being applied in a similar broad sense under the New Covenant - See Ephesians 4:25, which quotes Zechariah 8:16 and Romans 7:7, which quotes Deuteronomy 5:21.

A broad Old Testament command being applied to a wider group of people under the New Covenant... Ephesians 6:2-3 reapplies Exodus 20:12, to the broader context of all believers in all countries. In its original context, however, Exodus 20:12 related only to Israelites living in the Land of Canaan.

The broadening of the commandment of Exodus 20:12 occurred only because of the changeover from the Mosaic Covenant to the New Covenant. The Mosaic Covenant was given to the Jews, but the New Covenant was given to both Jews and Gentiles (see Leviticus 26:46, 27:34, Romans 2:14, 9:4, Galatians 3:28 and Colossians 3:11).

Broad commands reapplied to new specific New Covenant contexts - Examples of these are found in Acts 13:47, 1 Corinthians 5:13, 6:16, 2 Corinthians 10:17 and 13:1.

In 1 Corinthians 5:13, Paul applies the broader command of Deuteronomy 17:6-7 to the specific sin of incest at the Church at Corinth. Deuteronomy 17:6-7 commands: ***"Whoever is worthy of death shall be put to death on the testimony of two or three witnesses, but he shall not be put to death on the testimony of one witness. The hands of the witnesses shall be the first against him to put him to death, and afterward the hands of all the people. So you shall put away the evil person from among you."*** Note Leviticus 18:8 reveals that having incestuous sex with your father's wife is sin. Also, observe Leviticus 18:29 shows those who committed the sin of incest under the Mosaic Covenant would be ***"cut off from"*** God's people.

In 1 Corinthians 6:16, Paul quotes God's broad command found in Genesis 2:24 and reapplied it to the new specific situation of a person having sex with a prostitute. In 2 Corinthians 10:17, Paul states: ***"But He who glories, let him glory in the Lord."*** Here Paul quotes the broad command of Jeremiah 9:24: ***"But let him who glories glory in this, that he understands and knows Me…"*** In the context of 2 Corinthians 10:17, Paul applies the command of Jeremiah 9:24 in relation to the specific matter of ministering for Jesus Christ.

In 2 Corinthians 13:1, Paul quotes the broad command of Deuteronomy 19:15 and applies it to his specific situation. 2 Corinthians 13:1 states: ***"This will be the third time I am coming to you. 'By the mouth of two or three witnesses every word shall be established.'"*** Deuteronomy 19:15 commands: ***"One witness shall not rise against a man concerning any iniquity or any sin that he commits; by the mouth of two or three witnesses the matter shall be established."***

All believers need more wisdom and knowledge from the Biblical Scriptures of God. **(Read Proverbs 1:20-2:22, 4:7-13, 5:1, 10:21, Philippians 1:9 and Colossians 1:9).**

1 Corinthians 1:24 and 30 reveal *Jesus Christ is our wisdom* from God. In Colossians 2:3, Paul says that in Christ ***"are hidden all the treasures of wisdom and knowledge"***. Christ is God and therefore is the Source of all wisdom and knowledge. All Biblical, supernatural guidance and natural wisdom originate in Him.

Because Christ lives in us as believers, we have all His wisdom and knowledge in *potential* form within us. This does not mean we are God or know all His wisdom and knowledge. However, all His wisdom and knowledge are there ready to be communicated to us as He wills.

Galatians 2:20: "*I am crucified with Christ: nevertheless I live; yet not I, but Christ liveth in me: and the life which I now live in the flesh I live by the faith of the Son of God, who loved me, and gave himself for me.*"

Colossians 1:27: "*To whom God would make known what is the riches of the glory of this mystery among the Gentiles; which is Christ in you, the hope of glory:*"

As we meditate on His written Word (see Psalm 119:15, 27, 78 and 148) and have intimate fellowship with Jesus Christ through His Spirit **(read 2 Corinthians 13:14 and Philippians 2:1)**, He often will impart Biblical and supernatural guidance, wisdom, and knowledge to us. Fellowshipping with God through His Holy Spirit involves *sharing thoughts* and *feelings* with each other. Examples of this are found in Exodus 3:1-4:17 and Acts 9:10-17 when God and Moses and then God with Ananias shared their thoughts and feelings.

The written Word of God teaches there are basically 5 types of wisdom and knowledge:

- **Biblical**
- **Supernatural guidance**
- **Natural**
- **Worldly**
- **Devilish**

Biblical wisdom and knowledge is from God **(read 2 Peter 3:15-36 and 2 Timothy 3:15-16)**. Supernatural guidance wisdom and knowledge is from God through the voice and witness of His Spirit, dreams, visions, angels, His audible voice and signs in circumstances. Refer to **Job 33:14-16**.

God also gives much natural wisdom and knowledge to both believers and unbelievers. **Luke 11:31** uses the word ***"wisdom"*** partly to refer to God-given natural wisdom to Solomon. **Exodus 28:3, 31:3-6,** and **35:30-36:2** record's God giving natural skills, knowledge, and wisdom to His people. **Exodus 31:3-5 states:** *"And I have filled him with the Spirit of God, in wisdom, in understanding, in knowledge, and in all manner of workmanship, to design artistic works, to work in gold, in silver, in bronze, in cutting jewels for setting, in carving wood, and to work in all manner of workmanship. And I, indeed I, have appointed with him Aholiab the son of Ahisamach, of the tribe of Dan; and I have put wisdom in the hearts of all the gifted artisans, that they may make all that I have commanded you."*

These verses reveal that God-given natural wisdom and knowledge can be used under the *influence* and *oversight of the Holy Spirit*. Natural wisdom and knowledge can be obtained through the outworking of our natural God-given talents. Natural wisdom and knowledge can be learnt through reading, being taught by other humans, observing others using their God-given natural wisdom and knowledge, or us observing the natural world.

Nehemiah 2:11-16 records Nehemiah obtaining natural knowledge through observation. Abel used natural wisdom to look after sheep **(read Genesis 4:2).** Jacob used natural wisdom to dig a well **(read Genesis 26:22).**

Elisha used God-given natural wisdom involved in ploughing **(read 1 Kings 19:19). Acts 27:21-26** and **33-38** records that Paul received supernatural wisdom from God's angel and then used natural wisdom about the need to eat food. God has perfect knowledge and wisdom about all natural matters. As humans, we only have a limited knowledge and wisdom about the natural realm. The Bible also refers to the wisdom of the world, which is also called man's wisdom **(read 1 Corinthians 2:13)** or fleshly wisdom **(read 2 Corinthians 1:12)**. Worldly wisdom is different from natural wisdom and is not from God. **1 Corinthians 1:19-20 and 3:19-20** show the wisdom of the world is ***"foolishness"*** in God's eyes.

In **2 Corinthians 1:12**, Paul, the highly intelligent Apostle says he did not live by the wisdom of the world. **Acts 18:3** shows Paul made use of the God-given natural wisdom of tent making. However, the latter is different from worldly wisdom. Worldly wisdom originates from the pressuring system that tries to influence us to think in ways contrary to God's will as revealed in His Scriptures and by His Spirit. This pressuring system is what the Bible calls ***"the world"*** in verses such as **1 John 2:15-16**, **1 John 5:19** and **James 4:4.** The world as described in the New Testament is any non-Christian way of thinking and acting. Today it constantly uses other people, advertising, television, and education, to try in getting us to conform to it. It exists in different forms in different countries. An example of worldly wisdom is the theory that humans are born with a good nature. This idea is contrary to **Genesis 8:21**, **Jeremiah 17:9** and **Ephesians 2:1-3**. Devilish wisdom is written about in **James 3:14-16**. The verses show satanic wisdom will be somehow linked to various sins such as envy, selfishness, disorder and so on.

Occult, witchcraft, psychic practices, and the teachings of false prophets are other examples of devilish wisdom. Devilish and worldly wisdom are closely linked. The great difficulty every Christian faces is that the education system, newspapers, books, movies, news broadcasts, current affairs programs, computer discs and other means of communication are mixed with worldly and God-given natural wisdom together. Even the seemingly harmless management law and medicine courses at universities, mix God's given natural wisdom, with worldly and satanic wisdom. For example, many management courses put more emphasis on outward results than integrity. In many Western countries, maybe **50% –70%** or more of journalists, editors and television commentators, have no personal relationship to Jesus Christ.

As a result, their written or spoken words are often a reflection of the sins and satanic deception in their own lives. Satan uses these people to deceive their thousands of readers, or listeners about many things.

Natural God-Given Talents.

One unbiblical view teaches that our natural talents are all evil and to be suppressed. However, note in **Exodus 4:11**, God told Moses his mouth was God's gift. As stated before, Paul used his talent of tent making **(read Acts 18:3).** King David had God-given abilities in music **(read 1 Samuel 16:17-18)** and looking after sheep **(read 1 Samuel 16:11).** God gave the prophet Daniel natural skills in literature **(read Daniel 1:17).** So natural talents are God-given.

But our natural talents must be used in submission to the Holy Spirit **(read Romans 6:13, 6:19 and 12:1-2).** Paul, David, and Daniel were all surrendered to and led by the Holy Spirit.

In relation to David's plans, **1 Chronicles 28:12** refers to ***'the plans for all that he had by the Spirit'***. The Holy Spirit often led Paul, in his own life **(read Acts 13:1-3, 16:6-7, 16:9-10, 18:9-10, 19:21, 20:22-24 and 22:17-21).**

One Kings 4:29-34 records the awesome wisdom God gave King Solomon. As Solomon was the wisest person in history **read 1 Kings 3:12 and 4:31.** God gave him awesome wisdom about natural and spiritual matters **(read 1 Kings 4:29-33)**. Solomon received this wisdom without doing university courses or scientific research and without Solomon necessarily being born with a brilliant mind.

However, after Solomon received this massive impartation of wisdom from God, he followed his own human reason and common sense, by deciding to marry pagan foreign wives and concubines. **1 Kings 11:1-4 records:** *"King Solomon, however, loved many foreign women besides Pharaoh's daughter Moabites, Ammonites, Edomites, Sidonians and Hittites. They were from nations about which the Lord had told the Israelites, 'You must not intermarry with them, because they will surely turn your hearts after their gods.' Nevertheless, Solomon held fast to them in love. He had seven hundred wives of royal birth and three hundred concubines, and his wives led him astray. As Solomon grew old, his wives turned his heart after other gods, and his heart was not fully devoted to the Lord his God, as the heart of David his father had been."*

These foreign wives led Solomon into setting up altars in Jerusalem for pagan gods like Molech and Chemosh **(read 1 Kings 11:7)**. The worship of Molech and Chemosh involved human sacrifice and other evils. Despite having so much God-given wisdom, Solomon made many wrong decisions about marrying pagan foreign wives and concubines.

Joseph had earlier married an Egyptian wife. However, it is possible to argue Solomon's first marriage, was questionable, considering Egyptians were usually pagans. **1 Kings 3:1** seems to suggest Solomon married her to seal a political treaty with Pharaoh, king of Egypt. These type of human reasoning decisions, were all in disobedience to God's commands about Israelite kings not marrying many wives **(read Deuteronomy 17:17)** and about Israelites not marrying Moabites, Ammonites, Hittites and Canaanites **(read Exodus 34:11-16, Deuteronomy 7:1-4 and 23:3-6).** Note the women of Sidon whom Solomon married were Canaanites. Refer also to Nehemiah 13:1-3 and 13:23-27.

This now leads me on to testimonials... It is good to be inspired by testimonies of God miraculously working in people's lives. Such testimonies are often practical revelations of God's wonderful character. But we must also be very careful when listening to or reading testimonies. Testimonies are sometimes used in preaching and in books to give supposed credibility to various unbiblical teachings and practices. Among some churchgoers in the early Christian centuries, some testimonies about miracles became oral traditions, which were used by the Devil to deceive later generations.

I have heard some modern Charismatic preachers use testimonies of miracles, which they claimed occurred previously in their own ministries in order to gain supposed credibility for their own unbiblical teachings and their focus on emptying the wallets of their listeners. Testimonies about miraculous events supporting unscriptural ideas are called fables. In the New Testament, the word "***fable***" is used in **1 Timothy 1:4, 4:7, 2 Timothy 4:4, Titus 1:14 and 2 Peter 1:16.**

In Greek, the word "***fable***" is "muthos" which means "a legendary story or account, normally about supernatural beings, events or cultural heroes, and in the New Testament always with an unfavourable connotation".

In **2 Timothy 4:3-4**, Paul prophesied a future time or times when many churchgoers would not like sound Biblical doctrine would be turned aside by false teachers to religious fables.

In other words, Paul predicted by the Holy Spirit that in the future many churchgoers would focus on dramatic testimonies about miracles, which would teach things contrary to the Scriptures. Paul did not oppose casting out demons, angelic visitations, healings, miracles and revelations of the Holy Spirit. But he did oppose any testimony about these things, which suggested anything contrary to the sound doctrines of the Word of God. Most modern preachers of miraculous fables, or miraculous testimonies, which support unscriptural ideas and practices, make fun of those who emphasise the importance of sound Biblical doctrine. But note in 2 Timothy 4:3, Paul identifies such opposers of sound doctrines as false teachers.

In Titus 1:9, Paul emphasised the importance of church leaders preaching sound Biblical doctrine: "***holding fast the faithful word as he has been taught, that he may be able, by sound doctrine, both to exhort and convict those who contradict.***" In 1 Timothy 4:6, Paul stated one of the qualities of being a good minister is following good doctrine: "***If you instruct the brethren in these things, you will be a good minister of Jesus Christ, nourished in the words of faith and of the good doctrine which you have carefully followed.***"

In **Titus 1:14**, Paul warned the Apostle Titus to not listen to testimonies about miraculous events and supernatural beings, which suggested unbiblical ideas: "***not giving heed to Jewish fables and commandments of men who turn from the truth.***" Paul here linked such fables with man-made religious commandments. The history of the church records many examples of miraculous fables being used to support man-made religious laws.

In **2 Peter 1:16**, Peter insists he and the other Apostles did not follow cleverly devised fables, or false miraculous testimonies when preaching about Jesus Christ:

"***For we did not follow cunningly devised fables when we made known to you the power and coming of our Lord Jesus Christ, but were eyewitnesses of His majesty.***"

If a man of God stated: "Last night, God gave me a dream in which He revealed to me that it is impossible to be accepted into His Presence in Heaven, unless we give His ministers very expensive gifts. He told me proof of this is that the wise men were only allowed into Jesus' Presence after His birth, because they bought gifts of such great value." Such a fabled interpretation of **Matthew 2:1-2** and **7-11** is a form of legalism, by which eternal salvation is supposedly partially merited by giving money. Note: God said in **Deuteronomy 10:17** that He never accepts bribes or money gifts which try to manipulate Him. Jonathon Edwards was one of the leading preachers in the Great Awakening revival, which occurred in the United States in the 1700's. He wrote: "We know what the apostle means by 'the world' or 'the things that are of the world' from his own words in chapter 2:15,16 'Do not love the world or anything in the world. If anyone loves the world, the love of the Father is not in him. For everything in the world – the cravings of sinful man, the lust of his eyes and the boasting of what he has and does – comes not from the Father but from the world.' Plainly, he means everything to do with sin and includes all men's corruptions and lusts, everything they look to for satisfaction. Therefore, from what the apostle says here we may safely conclude that if a people:

1.Have their love of ordinary, worldly pleasure, profits, and honors lowered.

2.Are weaned from eagerly chasing such things.

3.Have a deep concern about eternity and the eternal happiness that comes through the gospel.

4.Earnestly begin to seek God's kingdom and righteousness.

5.Are convicted of the ugliness and guilt of sin, as well as the misery to which it leads. - Then the Spirit of God must be at work.

A man with an awakened conscience is the hardest man in the world to fool! The more awake a sinner's conscience is, the harder it is in quietening it down until it is really delivered from sin. The more a conscience is aware of the greatness of man's guilt, the less likely he is to be satisfied with his own righteousness. Once a man is thoroughly frightened by a sight of his own danger, he will not believe himself truly safe without good grounds. Awakening a conscience in this way is not likely to confirm a man in his sins; on the contrary, it is likely to lead to sin and Satan driven out. So, whenever we see people made aware of:

1.The dark side of sin.
2.God's anger against sin.
3.Their own natural lost-ness because of sin.
4.Their own need of eternal salvation.
5.Their needs of God's mercy and help.
6.Their need to do what God has commanded in seeking salvation.

"We may certainly conclude that it is the Spirit of God at work!" Edwards also wrote:

"When man are persuaded to love the Holy Scriptures more, and trust their truth and divine origin more, it is certainly the Spirit of God at work. This is the sign the apostle gives to all of us: "It has often happened in history that many sects of enthusiasts have undervalued the written word of God. They set up some other authority, which is over the Scripture. That still happens today. But when men come to value the Scriptures more and not less, then the Spirit of God is certainly at work."

I am so glad to feel God's Spirit work inside of me knowing that God will be there to help me in all of my life trials. He has given me a fresh start in life for everything that I have prayed for; a new beginning in America, a wonderful wife that is loyal, supportive and loving, a baby girl with blond hair and blue eyes and with another baby blessing on the way. With God on my side, I am humbly motivated to succeed in life through His Words. Over the years, I know what it feels like to be without God and His leadership in my life. I truly praise God for all my endeavors.

Praise Be In The Name Of God Our Father, The One True God.

I would like to take this opportunity to ask Jesus in blessing you in your walk with God and in turn would like to thank you, for taking time in reading my testimonials and God's Word for all our lives.

A Very Special Thanks - To God who has inspired and blessed me with the gifts to write this book, my wife Angela who brought me closer to God, my mentor and earthly father Michael, that has always inspired me throughout my business and personal life. Not forgetting my mother that born me. Finally to a wonderful, caring loving nan "grandma", (Nancy Rose Blackman) that I love so dearly; who helped raise me in my younger days to be confident in the Lord.

Andrew Feehily – Book Author.

INDEX TO BOOK

LET"S MOVE MOUNTAINS.
Introduction. 4

WORDS ARE LIFE ITSELF.
Controlling Our Words. 8
Business Loss Through Words. 14
We Have A Loss Of Light. 15
We Have A Loss Of Joy. 16
We Sustain A Loss Of Peace. 17
We Experience A Loss Of Love. 17
We Suffer A Loss Of Fellowship. 18
We Loss A Loss Of Confidence. 19
Knowing God Through His Words. 21
God Uses Ordinary People. 25
Understanding The Mystery Of God's Word. 27

BELIEVE YOU CAN SUCCEED& YOU WILL.
What You Say Is What You Get. 29
My First Impression Of Life. 30
Jesus & The Centurion. 41

SPIRITUAL ROADBLOCKS.
Jonah's Roadblocks. 46
The Holy Spirit. 51
Finding An Angel. 53
Talking To Jesus. 55
Dreaming Of Jesus. 57

STRUCTURE FOR SUCCESS.

Faith, Belief & Obedience. 64
Heaven & Mr. Jack Bean. 66
Does Hell Exist? 76

GOD & HIS PROPHESIES.

The Truth Behind The Bible. 82
Prophecies Concerning Jesus. 98
Jesus' Promises To All Of His Followers. 105
Background To Jesus. 111
The Records Of Jesus' Supernatural Acts. 112
The Main Witnesses Of Jesus. 113
The Breakdown Of The Bible. 114

LIFE CHANGING SCRIPTURES.

God's Inspiration. 122
When I'm At Wits End. 123
When I Need Assurance That God Is There. 124
When Everything Goes From Bad To Worse. 126
When I Feel Like Giving Up. 127
When I Need Both Help & Hope. 128
When I Worry About The Future. 129
When I Face Opposition. 130
When I Need To Know Right From Wrong. 131
When I Have Sinned. 131
When I Need Strength. 132
When I Am In Trouble. 133
When I Am Fearful. 134
When I Do Not Know Which Way to Turn. 135
When No One Seems To Care. 135

MOVE MOUNTAINS WITH PRAYER.

When You Pray, Pray In The Spirit. 138
Do People Get Healed Through Prayer? 139
Answers To Prayer In Faith. 140
Praying With Confidence. 141
Do You Pray Enough? 142
Be Honest When Praying. 145
Jesus Tells Us How To Pray. 150
Living A Christian Life. 152

(All scriptures are from the King James Version and the New International Version.)